Life Choices

Getting Your Financial Act Together

by Dr. Richard and Dawn Bence

LIFE CHOICES
Copyright © by Richard and Dawn Bence

All rights reserved. No part of this book may be reproduced or transmitted in any form by any means, electronic or mechanical, including photocopying, recording or by any information storage or retrieval system — except by a reviewer who may quote brief passages in a review to be printed in a magazine or newspaper — without written permission from the Publisher.

EMPIRE COMMUNICATIONS CORPORATION
5818 N. 7th Street, Suite #103
Phoenix, Arizona 85014

First Printing: 1989

Although the Author and the Publisher have exhaustively researched all sources to ensure the accuracy and completeness of the information contained in this book, we assume no responsibility for errors, inaccuracies or omissions. Any slights of people or organizations are unintentional. If advice concerning tax, legal or related matters is needed, the services of a qualified professional should be sought. This book is not intended as a source of legal, accounting or financial advice.

ISBN 0-943529-04-2

Price: $12.00
    Additional Copies may be ordered for $12.00 each plus $1.50 Shipping/Handling from the Publisher.

PRINTED IN THE UNITED STATES OF AMERICA
by: General Graphics and Printing, Inc.
    10027 N. 19th Avenue
    Phoenix, Arizona 85021

Author's Acknowledgements

We would like to acknowledge our parents, Blanche T. Bence, Jerome A. Bence, Stella M. Rodman and Frank G. Rodman, who encouraged us to establish social and financial values. We would also like to thank Sherri Bence whose careful and thoughtful critique of the manuscript insured its appropriateness for young adults.

TABLE OF CONTENTS

			Page
Chapter	1	Finding The Future	1
Chapter	2	Making The Concept Of Free Choice Work For You	3
Chapter	3	Critical Differences	7
Chapter	4	Money Differences	11
Chapter	5	Your Winning Game Plan	15
Chapter	6	Financial Future Choices	19
Chapter	7	The Financial Choices	29
Chapter	8	Time Choices	33
Chapter	9	More Money Choices	39
Chapter	10	The Role Of Education	65
Chapter	11	Learning To Learn	67
Chapter	12	Career Choices	79
		Authors' Afterword	81
		Quotable Quotes	83

Chapter 1
FINDING THE FUTURE

Many people step forward to find the future only to discover they lack the maps and navigational know-how to get there!

To evaluate the need for a book of practical facts about success, personal finance, personal growth and career development, we interviewed two groups of people.

The first group consisted of men and women who, without any particular advantages in family background, had achieved above-average success in their careers or businesses. The questions we asked can be summarized as: *"When and how did you decide to be a high achiever?"* Without exception, they listed the information contained in Section One of this book as the launching pad for their commitment to excel. Although they acquired this information in different ways, at different times, it was this information that got them going in a positive direction.

The second group we interviewed was made up of young adults who had graduated from high school within the last several years. They were asked what they needed to know and would like to know about career, finance and success matters. Their answers can be summarized as: "Everything!" Most had completed their years in high school without gaining preparation for successfully making career decisions, managing money or organizing their efforts to achieve specific goals. And, unfortunately, most of them had no idea where to find this kind of information.

We are disturbed by all this, for an obvious reason. I have three successful careers; I am an endodontist in private practice, an active writer and a Registered Representative for the sale of securities. My wife owns a small business and is a property manager and homemaker. We have done, and continue to do, very well financially and enjoy a great lifestyle. But that is less a virtue of our specific careers than it is a result of understanding and applying certain fundamental principles of successful living that go undiscovered by the overwhelming majority of people.

Nearly everyone we know *wants* "more." More satisfaction, more love, more of the American Dream. To settle for less is to be less! Here, in the wealthiest and most productive society in all of history, surrounded by opportunity, there are many people who settle for much less than they could have and be, and would like to have and be.

Newcomers to our society are appalled at the apathy of those people who choose not to strive for everything that is available to them.

Look around. You will certainly see some people who are enjoying the present and creating the future. People with exciting goals, interesting occupations, past-times and positive attitudes. You will also see a greater number of people with passive lives, accepting whatever occurs, living only vicariously through the television. It's important to compare these approaches because you have the opportunity to choose which way you will approach life. And, failure to make the choice is a choice.

Don't Stop Dreaming — Start!

We should have what we want. When you express your ambition, many people will tell you to stop dreaming. They want to force their very limited idea of "reality" on you and everyone else around them. However, to a great degree, you can create the reality of your choice.

To get what you want, you have to begin by controlling your thoughts. We become what we think about! It's not difficult to know, at least in general terms, the nature of a person's thoughts once you understand that the person is what he thinks. This makes mind-reading easy!

Presidents and millionaires and winners think about different things than laborers, poor people and non-achievers. The winners' thoughts did not suddenly become the thoughts of great men and women. The winners became great because their thoughts and dreams were those of great men and women.

Remember any childhood dreams? Prince, princess. Movie star. President of the United States. For a brief time, you may have imagined these to be real. You also had other, even more attainable dreams. Your own home, a great sports car, a trip around the world.

You may have heard of John Goddard. He has occasionally appeared on television talk-shows or been featured in national magazines in connection with one dramatic accomplishment or another. When still a young boy, John Goddard sat down and made a list of hundreds of things he wanted to do and places he wanted to go. Big things, like becoming a millionaire, being a big game hunter. Little things, like learning to touch-type. He has spent his life achieving these goals.

The only difference between John Goddard and many others is that John took his dreams seriously. Winners and losers share the ability to dream. Winners and losers may often share the same dreams. Winners learn to support their dreams with determination, organization and positive action.

Dreaming is the first step to getting what you want.

Chapter 2
MAKING THE CONCEPT OF FREE CHOICE WORK FOR YOU

We have the choice of pursuing our dreams or not dreaming at all. Many people deny this concept of free choice. But there are millions of people who are making that choice.

This concept does not mean that every poor and uneducated person chooses to remain poor and uneducated. Many such people are trapp'ed by their environment. They may have had their dreams and determination severely oppressed. They may have no belief in the concept of free choice.

Most of these people could do something to improve their own circumstances if their dreams were re-kindled and their determination strengthened.

You are probably not struggling with such dire circumstances. You are probably not severely oppressed. You are subject, though, to overlooking the application of free choice in your life. Millions simply *neglect* to make choices that will lead to productive and happy lives.

Certainly, if I had not made the choices I made, my life and the life of my family would be very different today.

You probably have fewer obstacles to overcome than many people in your community. Yet, it is the successes of the severely handicapped and the oppressed that verify the opportunity to be successful exists for anyone, everyone, for you.

How about the young man whose face was so terribly disfigured in an attack by a bear that years of corrective surgery still left him suicidal — but he got himself together and became a top insurance salesman in Canada. Or another young man permanently confined to a wheelchair by a high school trampolene accident who still built a huge international business. Or the girl who lost a leg in a car accident who still became an Olympic-competing skier. These are just a few of hundreds of examples we know of and, undoubtedly, tens of thousands of people who have refused to let physical handicaps rob them of full, successful lives.

Are You The Advantaged Or Disadvantaged?

The truly advantaged person grew up in a family of winners. He was surrounded by people who made a practice of gettting what they wanted out of life and knew how to help others do the same.

Too many people grow up surrounded by people who rarely got what they really wanted from life and had no clear idea of how to go about changing that pattern. These people, understandably, become cynical, critical, skeptical and negative. They discourage their children and their friends from pursuing "the good life" because they honestly feel it is unavailable. Sometimes, they resent those who insist on pursuing bigger and better than average goals.

If you grew up in the second type of environment, it's now up to you to do something about it. *You* have the choice of being controlled by it or out-performing it.

Winners choose an environment populated by winners. If parents, teachers, friends do not encourage the pursuit of exciting, meaningful dreams, then you must seek out a new collection of friends and associates who will encourage you.

You must learn to recognize, listen to, respect and emulate people who clearly know how to succeed.

It's important to note that you do not need to stop loving and respecting members of your family to look elsewhere for leadership. People can be good, honest, hard-working; have virtues without knowing how to succeed. People can deserve your love and respect as parents, grandparents, teachers or just as "elders" without being continuing role models for you.

Don't Just Look To Others. Look Inside.

Each of us has a unique kind of genius. The problem is that we are often conditioned to suppress and under-value that genius.

Suppose you were raised in an environment where creativity, exploration and personal growth were always encouraged. Where every accomplishment was celebrated! Would you question your abilities? You would accept success as a way of life. You would be filled with optimism.

If you have not had that kind of experience, the fact still remains that you have tremendous ability. You have abilities *and* opportunities! Now the challenge is to identify them.

Fortunately, we live in a Free Enterprise System. This is a System that benefits everybody. It permits each person to be rewarded in proportion to the abilities and opportunities he can identify, to the goals he can set and accomplish.

The Era Of Opportunity

As we write this book, we believe that our society is entering an exciting new era; an era that historians will look back on as a time of incredible opportunity; a time when people re-discovered the real meaning of our Free Enterprise economy.

This is a time of which you can take advantage. The beginning steps are very simple:

3 STARTER STEPS

1. *Find five successful people you respect and with whom you can spend time.* Ask these people about their early dreams and plans, problems and discouragements they encountered and overcame, methods they used to motivate themselves. Learn from these examples.

    Remember: most successful people have been inspired by others. You'll discover that those you consult will tell you about others who inspired them. You'll see that, by taking this step, you are placing yourself in a continuing chain of successful achievement.

2. *Make a practice of reading books that further convince you of the unlimited opportunities all around you and your ability to capitalize on them.* These can be self-improvement books, like this one, or biographies and autobiographies of successful people who interest you.

    One such book that is very important to read is *JONATHAN LIVINGSTON SEAGULL*, by Richard Bach. You can read this unusual little book in just one sitting. Through the parable of a seagull who appeared to be very ordinary but became extraordinary in the face of insurmountable odds, the author illustrates the value and power of a dream.

3. *Begin clarifying what you really want.* Surprisingly, most people never discover and identify what they really want. You will either determine your future or have it determined for you by people who care much less about you than you do!

Chapter 3
CRITICAL DIFFERENCES

One excellent way to learn how to be successful is to examine the differences between other successful and unsuccessful people.

One such difference has to do with expectations. In sports, in business and in life, winners actually expect to win!

Those who expect victories are surprisingly undiscouraged by failures. Their normal reaction to an apparent failure is to redouble their efforts. If things don't work out as planned, they still do not abandon their original choices.

Thomas Edison had over 1,000 inventions that can generally be considered successful, although some have proven more successful than others. But Edison also had many thousands of failures. Many thousands of ideas in which Edison invested time, energy and emotional commitment never collected a single dividend.

Famous "Home Run King" Babe Ruth actually had more strike-outs than home runs in his career.

It's important to note that these people are known for their successes, not their failures. You, too, can and will experience more strike-outs than home runs enroute to achieving your major goals. But, when you persist and win, you'll be known as a winner. And you'll have the rewards of a winner.

What Have You Prepared For?

Hand-in-hand with positive expectation goes positive preparation. Successful people actually *plan* their sucesses.

Most people pretty much go through life just letting things happen to them. Their planning is confined to relatively minor matters: a weekend activity; a vacation; a project to be done around the house.

Successful people plan those kinds of things, too, but they also plan all the important things in their lives. They develop career plans, savings plans, investment plans and business plans.

These people are not "pollyanna-ish" in planning, either, as some cynics like to believe. Successful achievers are realistic in their appraisal of the things they must do in order to see their plans through to accomplishment. Instead of being discouraged by a lengthy list of steps that must be taken, though, they are enthused and optimistic about the journey as well as the destination.

The Controversial Idea Of 'Mind Power'

There are many commonly used terms to describe the constructive use of the mind: *Positive Thinking* — coined by Dr. Norman Vincent Peale; *Possibility Thinking* — coined by Reverend Robert Schuller; *Positive Mental Attitude* — coined by self-made millionaire W. Clement Stone. And there are many philosophies and types of training that are either wholly or partially based on this same idea, including Silva Mind Control, EST, Mind Dynamics and Mind Science.

The world is just about over-flowing with critics of this idea. Some call it "simplistic." Others: "unrealistic." And the list goes on.

However, the principle is very sound. Even William James, a prominent Harvard University philosopher, noted, "The greatest discovery of our generation is that we can control our lives by controlling our attitudes."

If we can control our thoughts, we can control our lives. We become what we think about.

Although this idea is simple, it is not easy to apply. Controlling our thoughts requires training and concentration. An exercise that demonstrates this difficulty is: go stand in the corner for five minutes and think of anything *but* a pink elephant in a rocking chair. You won't be able to keep that darned elephant out of your mind!

Successful achievers, in every field, discover the value of controlling their thoughts and then succeed by doing so.

Some use "tools" for this purpose. Many use self-improvement and motivational audio-cassettes. For example. NFL quarterback Steve DeBerg is said to walk around with a portable cassette player hooked on his belt, headphones on, a motivational cassette playing. Some people use meditation, biofeedback, visualization and positive affirmations.

NBA star Larry Bird, the Celtics' perennial leader, says that he focuses on a mental picture of hockey great Bobby Orr immediately before each game and thinks of the qualities of Orr: courage, determination, 110% commitment. By doing so, Bird is using a technique to control his thoughts. While a player on the opposing team may be worrying, questioning his ability or thinking about a nagging pain, Larry Bird is focusing on positive characteristics of a champion he respects and admires.

You can learn to use your own mind to your advantage, as a motivational influence, with techniques like these. Different techniques work better for different people, so some experimentation is in order.

This is just another way of exercising freedom of choice. By choosing what you will think about most, you ultimately choose your education, career activities, relationships, even your income level and financial security.

The Good Advice Test

Good advice can save tremendous amounts of time and money. The quality of the advice you obtain can be a major factor in your success.

Poor advice has the opposite effect and can actually be worse than no advice at all!

Probably the worst advice I ever received was from a classmate in dental school who tried to convince me of the foolishness of working at a $3.00-an-hour job (in 1966) when a year or two later I'd be earning five times that much. He failed to value the financial and psychological benefits of remaining debt-free and of developing productive work habits. Fortunately, I resisted his influence and ignored his advice.

How do you judge the quality of advice?

We've developed a *4-Point Good Advice Test:*

1. *Is it TIMELY?* Advice must be useful in the future or potentially useful in the future. Advice that deals with the past rarely has any value.

2. *Is it APPROPRIATE?* Advice must be related to an objective you have set for yourself. If you've decided to create your own business, for example, advice urging you to get a secure job with a big company is inappropriate.

3. *Is it ACCURATE?* Advice should be based on valid knowledge, information or experience. This is what is meant by the saying "consider the source." Advice given by someone with no real qualifications for their opinion is dangerous.

4. *Is it POSITIVE?* There is no genius in devising ways that something *won't* work. Anybody can do that. The advice that has great value is that which points to the way something can be accomplished.

Learning to ask for advice is a winner's trait. Contrary to popular belief, most successful people are not arrogant egotists. Successful people seek out good ideas wherever they can be found. They are generally inquisitive and curious. They are generally good listeners.

Too many people either neglect or are afraid to ask for advice. This is a big error. Asking others for advice flatters them and demonstrates your willingness to listen to their ideas.

A Word About Work

Many people believe that hard work leads to success. Unfortunately success is *not* that simple. Look around — you'll find many hard-working people who are not particularly successful. Just working hard, as they do, will not lead to success. But there is a correlation between work and success. To be successful, you have to work very hard at being successful!

We might divide people into two groups: work-lovers and work-haters. There are work-haters all around you. These are the people who may work hard but have never learned how to work at becoming successful. Consequently, they don't see their efforts leading anywhere. The results of their work, as the old saying says, is "another day older and deeper in debt." Understandably, they grow to hate their work.

The work-lovers have a much different experience. First, they are good at what they do and excited about doing it. In fact, they often put in more time on the job or do more work than they are immediately getting paid for. These people find ways to direct their work toward well-defined goals. Sometimes this is called a "career path." *A person progressing from one point to another on a planned career path will, obviously, feel a lot better about work than the person just working to put food in the refrigerator each week.*

Successful people also invest some of their spare time in self-improvement and skill-improvement. They realize that what they do from five o'clock to midnight may be as important to their long-term success as what they do from "9 to 5."

You have to find and commit yourself to work that can lead you to exciting future goals and also be satisfying in the present. If you aren't in that position now, you have to wisely use your non-9-to-5 time to prepare yourself for such an opportunity.

They Call It "Big Mo"

Many athletes and coaches refer to "momentum" as "Big Mo." It's another way of acknowledging that "success breeds success."

As you understand and begin using one sound success idea after another, your attitude about yourself will become more positive. You'll grow more self-confident automatically and that's something exciting to look forward to!

Chapter 4
MONEY DIFFERENCES

In general, successful people have fewer money problems than unsuccessful people experience. This is because they make different fundamental choices about money. Successful people seem to adhere to four "Money Rules" that are pretty much ignored by the vast majority of people always struggling with money problems.

Rule #1:
Choose More, Not Less

Just about everybody starts out working to pay bills and provide the basic necessities of everday life. Unfortunately, many people get stuck there. Once they have established an acceptable lifestyle within their income, they stop striving for positive change. They get comfortable. They get defensive.

The successful person also uses his income to establish an acceptable lifestyle. But he never stops there. He spends only a limited time-span working just to pay the bills, then he moves on to work for lifestyle improvements, for investments, for financial security.

You have to determine what you are working for and for what you will work.

Rule #2:
Live With Real Economics

Financially successful people — *by definition* — spend less money than they take in.

For too many people, this is a shocking idea! All around them, they see people utilizing the liberal credit opportunities that are presently available to live beyond their means. What can't be seen, until it's too late, is the ultimate result of such an approach to life. The ultimate resut is a lifetime without any financial security. A lifetime of "running even faster to stay even."

Our government, too, has set a miserable example. They have gotten away with what Vice-President George Bush once called "voodoo economics" for so long that people no longer believe deficit spending has real consequences. We will pay the price for such sleight-of-hand in the future, probably through tax increases, bankruptcy of the Social Security System, and interest rates and inflation that may prevent an entire generation of ever owning homes or saving money.

This is certain: if you spend more money than you take in, you will inevitably suffer severely negative consequences.

One of the most important choices you will ever make is the one of behavior to perpetuate financial insecurity versus behavior that leads to financial security. And, regardless of your age, occupation or present financial circumstances, there is no better time than now to make that choice.

From as far back as I can remember, even as a child, I saved money. I believed that money was to be spent only when absolutely necessary. Such an attitude led me to always having more money than any of my friends. This reinforced my feelings and my goal of financial independence grew more and more believable to me. As a result, I have a life free of financial needs.

Successful people discipline themselves to save and invest first, then use the remainder of their income as wisely as possible; first for necessities, second for luxuries.

Here's an example of that discipline in practice:

When a person receives his wages, he first diverts a set percentage (2%, 5%, maybe even 10% or 20%) to build a secure financial future. This money may go into a savings account which will, in time, grow to sizeable proportions. Later, more sophisticated, higher yield options may be substituted for the ordinary savings account.

An individual with a $25,000.00 annual salary who places just 5% ($1,250.00) into his savings account each year, at only 5% interest, will have over $150,000.00 in that account in forty years. However, this will never happen unless that person puts that 5% into that account every time he gets a paycheck, without fail, no matter what! This is proved by the fact that 95% of all working people are chronically without cash or savings. They are no better off after forty years of work than after one year of work! Why? Because they spend their earnings first and try to save what's left over. If you are to develop financial security, you must do the opposite: save a certain amount, then spend the remainder.

Rule #3:
Handle With Care!

Successful people avoid going into debt unless it definitely improves their financial position.

Borrowing to pay for an education in order to achieve higher earnings over an entire career, for example, is often a good idea. Borrowing to purchase a home can also be a wise decision. At times, it may even be financially advantageous to borrow money and incur the cost of borrowing in order to invest the money at a greater return. Starting or investing in a business is a common situation of this type.

Most people get themselves deeply into debt for reasons much less defensible than these. In our "instant society", great caution must be exercised to avoid being so caught up in instant gratification that you become indebted for a lifetime!

Rule #4:
Be A Taxpayer, Not A Tax Victim

Taxes represent a huge expense to most individuals and families. In many cases, they combine into the largest category of expense with which you will deal.

Paying the taxes that you legitimately owe is proper, legally necessary and a reasonable response to the many opportunities, freedoms and services afforded to you by our government. Paying the appropriate taxes is patriotic. However, paying *more* taxes than you are legally required to pay is unnecessary and foolish.

The only way to be certain that you pay what you owe and not one cent more is to personally learn about and understand the tax laws, to keep accurate and complete records and to solicit qualified advice. That combination works. Abdicating the entire responsibility for determining your tax liability to someone else, though, usually results in your paying more than you need to pay. You may never know that is happening, but it will be.

Determined mastery of these four basic "Money Rules" can easily make a million-dollar difference in your financial circumstances during your career. It can, after only a few weeks, make the diference between feeling enslaved or feeling in control.

Every winner has a . . .

. . . game plan!

Chapter 5
YOUR WINNING GAME PLAN

The typical high school football coach invests more time in developing a game plan for one game, against one opponent, than most people ever invest in assembling a game plan for life.

Many people have an instant negative reaction to this idea of life planning. Just hearing the word "goal-setting" produces nervous apprehension and sweaty palms or honest but misguided skepticism.

Some people deliberately avoid selecting and defining goals because the process itself is difficult and challenging. Others avoid the process just because of the risk of subsequent failure.

Contrary to their reactions, successful business owners, executives, salespeople, doctors, lawyers, coaches, athletes, entertainment personalities and, probably, butchers, bakers and candlestick makers unanimously agree that learning to select and attain a goal is essential to success.

We are not trying, incidentally, to force our values on everybody else. There's really nothing wrong with going through life goal-less if you are satisfied with a static experience. This book was written for those who want a dynamic life experience badly enough to do something about it!

It's possible to go through school and even be well into your career without ever really learning how to set and achieve goals. The good news is that the process can be very simple.

Step One: Selection

One commonly used selection method is to sit down in a quiet place with pen and paper and write down the ideas that come to mind. A lengthy list can be compiled, then priorities selected.

One major goal may require the setting of lots of lesser goals. For a freshman college student to set a goal to be the dean of the law school in three years is ridiculous, but to set a goal to one day become dean and then set up a sequence of other goals to lead to that major goal is a good approach.

Another method is to define a lifestyle, then set goals that can provide that lifestyle.

Still another method is to ask: where would I like to be in one year, three years, ten years, longer? Looking years into the future can be helpful in goal selection.

Many times, you'll find that you cannot decide on a definite major goal without further thought, research, advice, even experience. Choosing a career or your retirement home and lifestyle may require more information than you possess right now. This should not be welcomed as an excuse for procrastination! You can still set some short-term and intermediate goals that will lead in positive directions.

It's important to work toward major goals even if they cannot yet be identified. With each step forward, we can see further!

Step Two: Action

When you select a goal, it is extremely important to do something about it immediately. Action prevents your commitment from weakening, your enthusiasm from dissipating. Action makes the goal real.

If you can do nothing stronger to get started, at least get the goal clearly put down in writing. Write the goal on several 3" x 5" cards and attach them to the bathroom mirror, sun visor in the car, etc., so that it can be seen frequently during the day. If the goal lends itself to a pictorial reminder, like a picture of a new car, so much the better.

Use these reminders to keep your mind on the goal. Thinking about the goal a lot will produce action steps you can take.

A simple physics demonstration of putting a rubber band around a heavy paperweight and pulling the band to move the paperweight across the desktop reveals that the band stretches more to start the movement than to keep it moving. More work is necessary to overcome inertia than to perpetuate motion. More effort is required to get going than to keep going.

Step Three: Systematic Progress

Each project has a beginning, a conclusion and some number of steps between. By analyzing a project, and breaking it down into sub-projects and small chronological steps, it becomes easier to tackle and becomes believable. The opportunity to accomplish a series of goals develops, putting momentum on your side.

We like to create and use simple Flow Charts for this purpose. Having a Flow Chart prevents the depression and confusion of not knowing what to do next.

Step Four: Work

It is important to understand that work is required to achieve most worthwhile goals. Often we have to give up leisure time in favor of accomplishing a particular goal. Several years ago, we gave up tennis — then a favorite pastime — to pursue a new goal. In three years, that goal was accomplished and time was again available for tennis.

Step Five: Commitment

Once we have decided on a goal, the challenge is to continually strengthen our commitment to it. Others will try and talk us out of it. When things are not going as we thought they would, we are vulnerable to others' negative suggestions. When the going gets tough, there is temptation to compromise or modify our goal to fit the limited progress we're experiencing. Understanding these temptations will help you resist them.

For some people, selecting goals but then failing to pursue them becomes a life-time pattern. This robs a person of accomplishment and everything that goes with it. People who frequently give up on the goals that are important to them can never have peace of mind.

Achieving a selected goal must be so important that we think of it often, see it in our minds clearly, even recite it aloud! Goals so energized with commitment tend to work like magnets; the more commitment given to them, the stronger they pull!

Congratulations!

Understanding this process for selecting important goals, and taking effective action to achieve them, is a giant step forward in everyone's life.

Now is the time to start using this process. We'd like you to delay reading further until you've selected one or more major goals, as we've discussed in this Chapter.

Chapter 6
FINANCIAL FUTURE CHOICES

Even the winner of the million dollars in the lottery had more than good luck. He had the initiative to purchase a ticket. Of course, we do not advocate basing your financial future on the lottery. But such an event still demonstrates that good things never just happen to us; we have to make them happen.

My daughter, at age 17, made an opportunity for herself to graduate from high school a semester ahead of schedule and then set up an aggressive curriculum so that she could graduate from college at age 19 (with straight A's). She has been accepted into a graduate studies program which will lead to a Ph.D. in clinical psychology. Her financial future is secure.

The choices I made at age ten, about saving versus spending, contributed significantly to my financial independence before age forty.

It is still amazing to us that so many people put more time, energy and effort into plannning a party or a vacation than they invest in planning their futures. Those who fit into this category have predictable financial futures, characterized by always spending more than they earn, always enslaved by debt, always playing "catch up", living from paycheck to paycheck, frighteningly vulnerable to unexpected expenses.

A very important financial future choice is the elimination or, at least, the reduction of financial worries and insecurity. This requires a plan, characterized by spending less than you earn, budgeting expenses, building cash reserves for savings and emergencies and getting and staying out of debt.

The people with chronic, lifetime financial problems believe that a shortage of money is the problem. That is simply not true. If it were, a cash windfall, such as a gift, an inheritance or a sweepstakes prize in excess of their debts would solve the problem permanently. However, in situations like this, the windfall is consumed and the financial problems reappear.

The key ingredient to successful financial planning is the determination to live with a plan. We will look at techniques of financial planning. First, though, let's look at the results by comparing the finances of two families. Their net incomes, expenses for necessities and net worths are identical. Both families encounter the same financial situations but they make very different choices.

(See Chart on next page)

5 YEARS OF FINANCIAL CHANGES	FAMILY "A"	FAMILY "B"
1st Year $100.00/month left after necessary expenses	$100.00 to savings	$100.00 to clothes, entertainment and miscellaneous items
2nd Year $100.00/month increase in net salary	$50.00 to IRA $50.00 cash reserve fund	$100.00 increase in car payments due to new car purchase and trade-in
3rd Year $5,000.00 inheritance	$5,000.00 mutual fund investment	$2,500.00 to savings $2,500.00 cruise vacation
4th Year $400.00/month (net) part-time job available to wife while children in school	$200.00 to IRA $100.00 to clothes, entertainment and miscellaneous items $100.00 to cash reserve fund	Choose not to work outside the home
5th Year $150.00/month increase in net salary	$ 50.00 to IRA $100.00 to mutual fund investment	$100.00 to clothes, entertainment and miscellaneous items $50.00 to savings

While the above table makes many assumptions, its intent is to provide a realistic comparison between two families with different financial goals.

Family-A chooses to retain their standard of living while discretionary income is used to create a more secure financial future. Family-B chooses to increase their spending to enjoy life more. (While it is likely that inflation would increase expenses for necessities, salary increases that are not listed would probably offset that factor.)

Calculations of increases in the two families' financial assets at the end of the five-year period *(as shown in the chart on the following page)* show an increase of $29,892.00 for Family-A but only an increase of $6,330.00 for Family-B. The difference is $23,562.00!

It's easy to see that the financial future of Family-B will be much different, much less secure than that of Family-A; not because of any shortage of money but purely because of the different choices made.

If these same situations re-occurred every five years for twenty years and the same basic choices were made, Family-A would have $286,378.00 more than Family-B.

FAMILY "A"

1st Year
$100/month to savings (at 4.5% for 5 years) .... $ 6,007.00

2nd Year
$50.00/month to IRA
— $600.00/year at 10% for 4 years 2,785.00
— $150.00/year tax savings .... 600.00 cash available
$ 50.00/month to cash reserve .... 2,400.00 cash available

3rd Year
$5,000 invested (in mutual fund) 6,475.00

4th Year
$2,400.00/year ($200.00/month) to IRA 5,040.00
(at 10%; invested at end of year)
Tax savings (IRA) .... 1,200.00 cash available
(2 years; 25% tax bracket)
$100.00/month to miscellaneous .... -0-
$100.00/month to cash reserve 2,400.00

5th Year
$ 600.00/year ($50.00/month) to IRA 600.00
(invested at end of year)
$1,200.00/year ($100.00/month) to mutual find
investment 1,200.00

Value of Investments $22,107.00
Cash Reserve 6,600.00
TOTAL $28,707.00
SPENT 2,400.00

FAMILY "B"

1st Year
$100.00/month to miscellaneous .... -0-

2nd Year
$100.00/month to car .... $ 3,000.00 increased value of car

3rd Year
$2,500.00 to savings .... $ 2,790.00
$2,500.00 to vacation .... -0-

4th Year
.... -0-

5th Year
$100.00/month to miscellaneous .... -0-
$600.00/year ($60.00/month) to savings 615.00

Value of Investments $ 6,405.00
Cash Reserve -0-
TOTAL $ 6,405.00
SPENT 11,500.00

— 21 —

Family "A" will have achieved, or almost achieved, a level of financial independence that guarantees the continuation of their standard of living without continuing to work. Family "B" will barely be able to see such a goal on a still distant horizon.

Achieving such financial independence, incidentally, is a very positive choice since most people eventually choose or are forced to retire from work and live on an income based on their investments plus whatever contribution may then be available from Social Security. Without the kind of financial independence we've described in this Chapter, you will almost certainly be compelled to live with a declining standard of living. Many of today's retirees made choices that led to exactly that fate.

It is painfully obvious that choosing to develop and follow a sensible financial plan is critically important.

The bare minimum financial plan should be to save at least a few dollars every week. While this doesn't sound like a very exciting, creative strategy, it will prevent "being broke" and it can create some financial security over many years. If a person born in 1925, for example, started working in 1945 and saved just a few dollars every week, he would accumulate over $40,000.00 in the insured safety of an ordinary savings account by 1990 at age 65. Although this is no fortune, it could spin-off about $400.00 a month in interest-income to supplement the Social Security and any pension benefits for which he might be eligible. Many retirees will tell you that an extra $400.00 a month of spendable dollars would make a big difference in their standard of living.

45 YEARS OF SAVING

Time Period	Amount Saved	Savings Account Interest Rate	Approximate Value In 10 Years	Approximate Value In 1990*
1945 through 1954	$ 3.00/week	2%	$ 1,642.00	$ 9,486.00
1955 through 1964	$ 5.00/week	4%	2,737.00	10,685.00
1965 through 1974	$10.00/week	5%	6,289.00	15,072.00
1976 through 1989	$15.00/week	6%	17,457.00	17,457.00
			TOTAL	$52,700.00

*assumes that all savings earned at the stated interest rate during each time period. (Any increase in the amount saved and/or a better average rate of return via investment diversification would produce a substantially greater total.)

This bare-minimum example serves to demonstrate that even a small savings habit can have a big lifetime impact, that what seems like a small choice now can lead to results of huge importance.

The following examples show how a person can proceed, step-by-step, to develop different levels of financial independence.

Step One:
Establish a personal net worth. List assets and liabilities. The difference is your net worth. Next, determine what you would like your net worth to be in one month, in one year and in five years. Be realistic. **Write down your projections.**

Step Two:
Determine what you are willing to do to achieve the financial goals listed in Step One.

Example: John

Situation
— age 19, single
— college student
— net worth: $2,600.00 in debt
— net income: $5,000.00 per year
— expenses: $7,500.00 per year
— available for savings: —0—

Immediate Goal
— continue academic achievements
— minimize indebtedness with part-time employment

Intermediate Goal
— acquire a master's degree by age 23
— pursue a career to eliminate debts and provide sufficient funds to live comfortably

Long-Range Goal
— (not known)

To achieve his goals on schedule, John intends to pursue a heavier-than-average academic schedule and carefully monitor his finances. His plan is simple and direct. Its success depends on his determination to see it through.

Example: Mary

Situation
— age 24, single
— secretary
— net worth: $ 5,000
— net income: $14.000/year
— expenses: $14,000/year
— available for savings: —0—

Immediate Goal
— establish a cash reserve fund
— purchase a new car
— visit friends in London

Intermediate Goal
— improve her income
— improve her work skills and abilities through formal education

Long-Range Goals
— marriage, family and career

To achieve her goals, Mary decreased her expenses by $5,000.00 per year by living with roommates rather than alone. Her new car, trip and cash reserve funds were then affordable. To improve her income, Mary knew that three years of evening classes would be required before she could attain a management position. Her eventual salary increase and additional education were in harmony with her long-range goals.

Example: Ed and Sally

Situation
— Age 25, married, 3 children
— laborer; mother and housewife
— net worth: —0—
— net income: $21,000.00/year
— expenses: $21,000.00/year
— available for savings: —0—
Immediate Goal
— buy a home
Intermediate Goal
— be able to finance college educations for the children
Long-Range Goal
— retirement without financial hardships

While Ed's and Sally's goals are few in number, their magnitude is great. With little chance of increases in income exceeding inflationary increases in expenses, it would appear that progress toward their goals will be difficult.

However, they realize that the only method of achieving their stated goals exists in some combination of salary increases through acquisition of a better paying job, additional part-time employment by Ed and/or Sally and by decreasing expenses. That may seem a bit simplistic but, barring some unlikely windfall of funds, it is the only solution.

It was determined that if Ed and Sally were willing to generate $5,000.00 per year in savings all of their goals could be achieved. To save $5,000.00 per year, Ed worked part-time weekends (8-10 hours) and Sally worked part-time evenings (10 hours per week). Together they earned $3,500.00 (net) per year. In addition, they carefully budgeted their expenses to reduce their expenses by $1,500.00 per year.

Example: Tom and Sandy

Situation
— age 40, married, 2 children
— executive; housewife and registered nurse (working part-time)
— net worth: $75,000.00

— net income: $55,000.00/year
— expenses: $50,000.00-$55,000.00/year
— available for savings: 0 to $5,000.00/year
Immediate Goal
— provide a college education for their children
Intermediate Goal
— improve their standard of living
Long-Range Goal
— none

Tom and Sandy should have little trouble achieving their goals, providing Tom's career continues to provide an increasing salary. In addition, Sandy will soon be relieved of her responsibilities, as a mother, as their children enter college. She will then be free to increase her earnings.

Step Three:
Re-evaluate progress annually. Often objectives change, opportunities arise and progress either exceeds or falls short of expectations.

One Year Later
John
  — academically on course
  — net worth: $5,000.00 in debt
  — goals unchanged
Mary
  — net worth: $8,000.00
  — purchased new car
Ed and Sally
  — net worth: $6,000.00
Tom and Sandy
  — no change

Five Years Later
John
  — graduated with master's degree
  — net worth: $15,000.00 in debt
  — net income: $17,000.00/year
  — repaying debt
Mary
  — married recently
  — net worth: $30,000.00 (Including husband's net worth)
  — net income: $22,000.00/year
  — available for savings (with husband's income): $10,000.00/year
Ed and Sally
  — net worth: $30,000.00
  — available for savings: $5,000.00/year
  — purchased a home
  — established college funds for children

Tom and Sandy
- unchanged (except slight increases in net worth, income and expenses)
- struggling to provide college education for children
- have an increasing awareness of the need for a retirement fund

Ten Years Later

John
- age 35, married
- net worth: $25,000.00 ($5,000.00 cash)
- available for savings: $5,000.00/year
- financial goal: financial security

Mary
- age 40
- housewife, mother and part-time career
- net worth: $75,000.00 ($25,000.00 cash), with husband
- financial goal: financial security

Ed and Sally
- age 41
- children in college
- purchased better home
- initiating a retirement fund

Tom and Sandy
- age 56
- unchanged (except slight increase in net worth, income and expenses)
- concerned about retirement income

At Retirement (age 65)

John was able to save $5,000.00 per year at a net annual rate of return of 8 percent. At retirement, his savings totaled over $600,000.00. The key to John's success was his ability to adjust his expenses so that each year $5,000.00 was available to save and invest.

Mary and her husband continued to be good money managers saving $8,000.00 per year, which earned 8 per cent interest (net) per year. At retirement, their retirement fund totaled over $750,000.00.

After Ed and Sally paid for their children's college education, they were finally able to upgrade their standard of living. They decided to place $2,500.00 per year, at 8 percent return, into an IRA which grew to $166,911.00.

Tom and Sandy were unable to change their spending habits and retired with a net worth of approximately $100,000.00 ($10,000.00 in cash). Fortunately, Tom had a pension plan that paid a monthly benefit.

The previous examples are fictitious but the situations, although sketchy, do occur. Those individuals, with goals and a plan to achieve them, live a life knowing that they will not be without the security that money provides. In the first three examples, the individuals developed the self-discipline to provide for their future before spending their money. They adjusted their incomes and their expenses so that they would never be poor.

Tom and Sandy, however, fell into the trap of satisfying their "wants" now and worrying about the future later. They lived to realize their error. At retirement, they were forced to reduce their standard of living considerably. Now, they must live their lives at the mercy of inflation, the economy and emergency cash needs. If they had saved and invested 10 percent of their net income from age 40 to age 65, their retirement fund (at 8% net return) would be valued at over $400,000.00.

Government statistics indicate that most people are broke at age 65. They are forced to rely on Social Security for their welfare. If they had placed just $5.00 per day in a passbook savings account, beginning at age 40, they would have over $87,000.00 in their retirement fund. If they started saving at age 30, the fund would have grown to nearly $165,000.00. It is our belief that many people are not aware of the importance of a consistent savings program. We hope that the examples in this Chapter help to clarify this important concept.

Chapter 7
THE FINANCIAL CHOICES

One character, in a comedy show, turned to the other and asked: "Can you remember exactly when and where you came to a split in the road; reality was to the right and you made a turn to the left?"

The underlying theme of everything we've talked about so far is that we are constantly presented with choices that must be made. Each choice is important in and of itself and in relationship to all other previous and subsequent choices. Choosing whether or not to use drugs, for example, at age sixteen will impact on the choices you can make and do make at age forty-six.

A good question to ask about every choice is: will this choice help me become the best person I'm capable of becoming and have the best life I'm capable of having?

There are Ten Financial Choices that seem to be made by all the successful, financially secure and financialy independent people we know.

Choice #1: Planning To Become Wealthy

We believe that everyone owes it to himself, his family and to society to accumulate the financial means to at least take care of his family's present and future needs and to make some contribution to the betterment of his community, state and nation. The person who can become wealthy and fails to do so by choice is no better off than a person hugely disadvantaged, maybe born in an undeveloped country, without real opportunity. Squandering opportunity is, we think, a sin.

It's important to understand that becoming wealthy does not necessarily require a huge income or a huge, one-time windfall of cash. We've shown that with a sensible plan, and the discipline to carry it through, a person of 'average means' can develop real wealth within their working lifetime — 40 years or less.

Choice #2: Learning To Become Wealthy

This book is not intended to complete your education in this area; it is intended to begin it! Imagine what you might do if you **had** to become wealthy — maybe under penalty of death or exile to hard labor in a Siberian coal mine. You would really study wealth! You would search for every book, every course, every article, every particle of information that might assist you. You would not procrastinate as so many people do. You would have a real sense of urgency. You would create and adhere to a plan.

In our society at least, there is no penalty of death or exile for the squandering of opportunity. However, approaching the subject and process of developing wealth as if there were such a penalty, will also free you from many other "slow death penalties" that do exist in our society. Learning to become wealthy can free you from debt, worry, stress, uncertainty, family discord, inadequate health care and many other negative situations.

Choice #3: Living On Less Than 100% Of Your Income

Saving 10% to 20% of your income will virtually guarantee the achievement of financial independence by or before retirement age. Spending 100%, or even 110%, of your income may provide some pleasant luxuries right now but will guarantee a very unluxurious lifestyle in the future.

If you choose to collect and study every published and recorded work on financial success there is, you'll find this idea in every single source: That you must pay yourself first, then pay your bills, then pay for luxuries.

25-Year-Old Worker Saving 10% to 20% Of His Income

Income	Percent Saved	Savings	Rate Of Return	Value At Age 65
$20,000/yr	10%	$2,000/yr	7%	$ 399,270
20,000/yr	20%	4,000/yr	7%	798,540
30,000/yr	10%	3,000/yr	7%	598,905
30,000/yr	20%	6,000/yr	7%	1,197,810

Choice #4: Developing A Cash Reserve Fund

Although we do not want to succumb to paranoiac worry about a myriad of disasters and emergencies that may occur in our lives, we also do not want to be wholly unrealistic in presuming we will go our entire lifetime without some unexpected, costly problem. The odds overwhelmingly favor each family facing one such crisis, if not more. A home fire, a burglary, a prolonged illness, an accidental death, a job layoff, even a business failure. Such things do not just happen to the other man's family.

In forty years of work, you'll receive about four hundred and eighty paychecks. Spending all the earnings, and living paycheck-to-paycheck, is as risky as many things you'd be very reluctant to do. It's a financial high-wire act without a net.

A good "safety net" is a cash reserve equivalent to about three months' earnings. The existence of this reserve fund provides lifetime protection against unexpected expenses rather than a lifetime of financial crisis without it.

Choice #5: Valuing Time

We've talked a great deal about money but little about its equivalent: time. Time at our work earns money.

If our services are worth $5.00 an hour, and we choose to work two hours extra for five days a week, we'll earn $2,500.00 extra each year. In just ten years, at 10% interest, our extra two hours per day has a value of nearly $40,000.00. The extra $10.00 a day doesn't sound like much but $40,000.00 extra sounds like a lot.

Time is also the ally of good investments. Time works hand-in-hand with money to create multiplied value. The earlier in life you begin investing, the better a friend time can be.

Investment	Years Invested	Rate Of Return	Value
$1,000.00	10	10%	$ 2,594.00
1,000.00	25	10%	10,835.00
1,000.00	45	10%	72,890.00

Choice #6: Practicing Financial Discipline

How many times have you made a New Year's Resolution and broken it the very next day? Did you know that on any given day over ⅔ of all adult Americans are starting a new diet? How many stick to it? Very, very, very few.

The value of the Financial Choices you make is controlled by disciplined follow-through. Skipping a day or two of saving, letting a paycheck slide by without saving — well, that may not seem like a very important thing right at the moment. But, as weeks become months that become years, the results are incredibly significant. The only sure path to financial independence is a financial discipline that permits no exceptions and no excuses.

Choice #7: Financial Priorities

At the beginning of this Chapter, we observed that life is a never-ending parade of choices. Making good choices consistently is very difficult without a governing set of priorities. Making good choices consistently becomes much easier with a governing set of priorities.

For example, making a certain minimum contribution to our savings each month is a very high priority with us. It governs many other decisions that confront us during the month. While this may seem a little restrictive, it actually guarantees the ultimate freedom: peace of mind.

Choice #8: Responsibility

When you blame other people or circumstances for your lack of progress, you give up control. This is the worst possible thing you can ever do to yourself. Pushing away the responsibility for a situation may temporarily let you feel better but it will make the situation worse and, if done as a pattern, will put the control of your life in the hands of others.

In almost every case, it really isn't our environment, another person or group of people or a combination of circumstances that control us; it is our reactions to those factors that count.

Choice #9: Planning For Retirement

If you are a young person, maybe a college student or recent graduate or even a teenager reading this book, the idea of retirement will probably seem unreal. It probably, hopefully, is a long way off. However, if you objectively think about it, you may spend as much as a third of your adult years "retired." Sadly, many people so stubbornly refuse to think about and plan for retirement that they are not financially, psychologically or emotionally prepared for it and almost instantly become ill or even die as a result.

The fact that retirement is many years away is a great advantage that you should exploit, not ignore. You have an opportunity to set in motion choices and disciplines to insure financial security at retirement age.

Why not be in the position to choose to keep working not because you must but because you really want to?

Choice #10: Start Now!

Many will read this book, nod in agreement, then put it on a shelf somewhere to gather dust. Be one of the few who take action on ideas and information to create a better life.

Chapter 8
TIME CHOICES

If most people pretty much squander money, which they do, they are even guiltier in squandering time. How many times have you heard someone say, often with a sigh, "Where does the time go?"

In life, there are no time-outs, no replays. Time steadily marches on without a pause, interruption or concern for any individual's use or misuse of it.

Successful achievers seem to share a special sense of time. They know, and frequently comment, that the past is gone, the future does not yet exist, that we live in the present. Dr. Edward Kramer, one of the earliest success philosophers and authors, wrote that "the only time is the NOW-time." W. Clement Stone, a self-made multi-millionaire who built a huge insurance company out of the depths of the Great Depression, says that the most positive statement in the world is: do it now!

This does not mean that we should live only for the present, ignore preparations for the future, neglect opportunities to learn from the past. Obviously that would contradict everything we've talked about so far. It simply means that the present moment is the only unit of time which we can use.

A recent behavioral study confirmed that the single, most significant characteristic of so-called 'high-achievers' is their ability or tendency to be totally engrossed in the now-situation until it is completed. They choose to focus totally and productively on one thing at a time, completing one thing after another.

The choices that we make about our moments, minutes and hours control the long-term value we get from months and years.

A very basic choice is to use or to waste time. We believe that appropriate use of time is doing anything which moves us closer to our pre-determined objectives. A certain amount of physical exercise and recreation is appropriate use of time in connection with our goals for physical fitness, good health and a positive relationship.

Waste of time is the aimless, pointless activity that has no definite connection to the achievement of goals.

There are seven more specific choices about time that can reduce waste, enhance productivity and accelerate progress toward goals.

Time Choice #1: Set Priorities

In a previous Chapter, we saw that a structure of Financial Priorities makes day-to-day decision-making easier. Having a structure of priorities for all aspects of life makes all sorts of decisions easier.

Time Choice #2: Combine Activities

We can't manufacture or find any more time but we can, sometimes, increase the value we derive from time.

We often listen to educational audio-cassettes while driving to and from the office or working around the house. This doubles the value of that time. A parent who works on cleaning out the garage, with the help of his son, not only gets the job done but also teaches work habits and ethics and spends meaningful time with the boy. That triples the value of that time.

The combining of activities happens sometimes by accident but can happen more through awareness and planning.

Time Choice #3: Control Television Viewing

"TV bashing" is a favorite activity of many self-improvement authors and lecturers. We do not agree. We enjoy television, often learn from television and believe it serves a very useful role in society. On the other hand, the people who flop in front of the TV, from arrival home at the end of the day until they doze off at 11:00 pm, are doing themselves a terrible disservice.

Selective, planned viewing of favorite shows for entertainment and special programs for education makes good sense. Indiscriminate viewing for hours and hours is a waste of time.

A Video-Recorder is an indispensable time-tool. With a VCR, you can record selected TV programs and view them at another, more convenient time.

Interestingly, the recorded programs are sometimes never watched as other activities take precedence. However, when they are watched at an ideal time, we've really exercised great control over our time rather than giving up that control to television programmers.

Time Choice #4: Set Aside Time For Recreation

All work and no play make Jack and Jill dull. Recreation is necessary for good mental and physical health, for good relationships with family and friends and as a reward for accomplishment.

Time Choice #5: Control Interruptions

Others will never value your time as you do. Others have their own agenda of priorities, probably not in perfect harmony with yours. Being able to politely, but firmly, say "no" is an important skill.

Time Choice #6: Schedule Activities

Many people contend that scheduling their daily activities is an infringement on their personal freedom. However, those people who make a practice of scheduling their daily activities will tell you that the process actually gives them more freedom. By helping them get more productive work done in less time, scheduling provides more time for social and leisure activities. By helping them progress toward goals more systematically and effectively, scheduling serves to ultimately enhance their incomes and net worths, again providing greater freedom.

Scheduling is really just an extension of setting goals and priorities. A goal can and should be divided into a list of sub-goals. These sub-goals can then be further divided into monthly, weekly, even daily tasks. These tasks can then be scheduled and given appropriate priority.

All of this planning, scheduling and organizing will, at first, seem complicated, maybe even intimidating. With a little practice, though, it becomes easy and the rewards so evident that we become eager to create daily schedules. Personally, there is no way that I could attend to my professional practice, my other business activities, my investments, my family and my leisure preferences without daily scheduling.

Scheduling your time will give you increased accomplishment, a great deal of personal satisfaction, greater control over your life and will make a positive contribution to career or business success.

Time Choice #7: Use Time Management Tools

There are many "time management systems", appointment books and planning calendars on the market, sold in office supply, stationary and book stores. Any of these are good, some are better than others, but all of them feature certain basic tools of time management.

The first basic tool is the WEEKLY PLANNER. This gives us a convenient place to write down our goals and planned activities for the week. Just writing them down strengthens our commitment to them. The WEEKLY PLANNER page that I use (see page 37) includes spaces to list my most important ten, five and one-year goals; the month's goals that will move me closer to the long-term objectives; places to list scheduled appointments for each day; then two to-do lists — one very important and the other of moderate importance. I also jot down things I'm going to do as rewards for completing the tasks I've assigned myself. Last, there's space for miscellaneous notes, ideas and items that need to be carried over to the next week.

The next basic tool is a THINGS-TO-DO-TODAY LIST of one kind or another. The format that I use is a DAILY SCHEDULE (see page 38) that has spaces to list each activity or task, approximately but not necessarily in priority order; then a 'Sequence Column', where I number them — 1 for the first to be done, 2 for the second, etc. This list may be built over a period of several days, then the sequential numbering done the night before or first thing in the morning. As I move from one completed activity to the next, I cross them off. There's also a column where I estimate the time needed for each task. And I rate each item 1, 2 or 3 for urgency and importance. This is helpful if conditions force the postponement of some tasks.

At the end of the day, a review of the DAILY SCHEDULE tells the story, clearly and accurately. It is a record of what has and has not been done. It is a confidence-builder, providing most or all of the listed activities that have been done. If you happen to be self-employed or in sales work, this record may someday come in handy in matching and justifying travel, entertainment and other expenses in a tax audit, too.

Use of these two, basic Time Management Tools alone will increase your overall productivity significantly. Most people find it "frees up" as much as an hour or two a day.

I have found that there is a definite correlation between having organized control over time and organized control over money. The two seem to go hand-in-hand.

WEEKLY PLANNER

MONTH _____

	SUN. ( )	MON. ( )	TUES. ( )	WED. ( )	THURS. ( )	FRI. ( )	SAT. ( )
APPOINTMENTS							
IMPORTANT							
LESS IMPORTANT							
REWARD							

GOALS

10-Year _____

5-Year _____

1-Year _____

Month _____

MISCELLANEOUS _____

"Character is the resolve to carry a project through to the end, even when the mood has left you!"

DAILY SCHEDULE

ACTIVITY	SEQUENCE	TIME NEEDED	IMPORTANCE
			1 2 3
			1 2 3
			1 2 3
			1 2 3
			1 2 3
			1 2 3
			1 2 3
			1 2 3
			1 2 3
			1 2 3
			1 2 3
			1 2 3
			1 2 3
			1 2 3
			1 2 3
			1 2 3
			1 2 3
			1 2 3
			1 2 3
			1 2 3

APPOINTMENTS:

Chapter 9
MORE MONEY CHOICES

In an earlier Chapter, we discussed Ten Financial Choices that, together, determine whether or not you will achieve financial security and independence within a reasonable length of time. In addition to these ten very fundamental choices, there are many, many more specific choices we make about money and about other things that directly affect our incomes and finances. In our research for this book, we talked to groups of young students as well as adults in various jobs, professions and businesses. They expressed these choices as questions, as answered here, to help you make the right money choices.

How Can I Earn Enough Money To Develop Wealth?

Actually, we demonstrated earlier that the level of your income is much less important than your uses of that income in developing wealth. However, it's obviously desirable to earn as good an income as you can.

The surest way to insure adequate earnings is to plan early in life to become capable of doing that which pays well. That's not the only factor that should govern your career choices, but it is an important one. I considered it in choosing my career.

Whatever career, profession or business you find yourself in, the quality of the job you do, and increasing your proficiency in that work, will, more often than not, lead to higher earnings and other opportunities. Most companies prefer to promote from within whenever possible.

Other than receiving money as a gift, there are two sources. The first is working for it and receiving it from a wage, salary or profits from owning your own business. The second source is to put money to work for us. Money in a savings account or some similar vehicle, for instance, is working for us.

One objective of saving and investing is to gradually increase the profits earned by the money so that we can decrease dependence on wages.

What Is "Net Worth?" How Do I Build It?

NET WORTH is the measure of your real wealth. It is calculated by subtracting all your current liabilities from the current liquidation value of your assets. Your assets may include cash, stocks and bonds, life insurance cash value, your home and other real estate, money owed to you, retirement funds (such as IRA's), your automobiles, collectibles and antiques, your home furnishings and other personal property. Your liabilities may include amounts owed on loans, credit cards and other bills, unpaid taxes, your mortgages and other debts.

It is, unfortunately, common for people to actually have "negative net worth"; to have their liabilities exceed the real value of their assets.

You build net worth by making the important, fundamental choices we've discussed throughout this book, notably including saving a portion of all your income. Home ownership is also a basic way to build net worth. Most financial planners urge buying the home you live in as a first, fundamental step in building net worth.

How Can I Get Out Of Debt?

The first part of the answer is a strong desire to be debt-free. This is a choice that requires real commitment because it is very easy to incur and accumulate debt in today's society. Presuming serious commitment, there are three steps to escaping from debt:

1. Stop doing whatever has created the debt. If it is living beyond your income or gambling or drinking — stop it immediately. If you have developed a serious addiction of one kind or another, face up to it and seek appropriate help. The shame is not in having a problem; the shame is in refusing to face it.

2. Devise a reasonable timetable to pay off your debts. Take a set amount of money from every paycheck you receive, and from all other money that comes to you, to make the planned payments.

3. Avoid all new debt unless it clearly improves your financial situation. For example, borrowing to purchase a home or invest in a business opportunity or education is probably positive.

Should I Pay Cash Or Charge It?

That largely depends on your level of discipline. We advise making purchases with credit cards only if you can and will pay the balance in full within thirty days. This is even better advice now that new tax laws have taken away the tax-deductibility of consumer interest. And, generally, the choice of having now but paying later erodes your self-control. An undisciplined consumer with credit cards can become a deeply indebted victim very quickly.

(See charts on next page)

Is It Better To Get A Tax Refund Or To Owe Taxes?

Eligibility for an income tax refund indicates that taxes have been overpaid, which means that the government enjoyed interest-free use of your money. If you owe taxes, you've had interest-free use of that money and can have invested it for profit.

Result of a continuous $500.00 balance on a bank credit card.

	Loan Balance	18% Interest Payments	Cumulative Cost
1st Year	$500.00	$90.00	$ 90.00
2nd Year	500.00	90.00	180.00
3rd Year	500.00	90.00	270.00
4th Year	500.00	90.00	360.00
5th Year	500.00	90.00	450.00

The five-year result is being $450.00 poorer and still $500.00 in debt. If the interest on the interest was not paid, the loan balance would increase to $1,143.88 in five years.

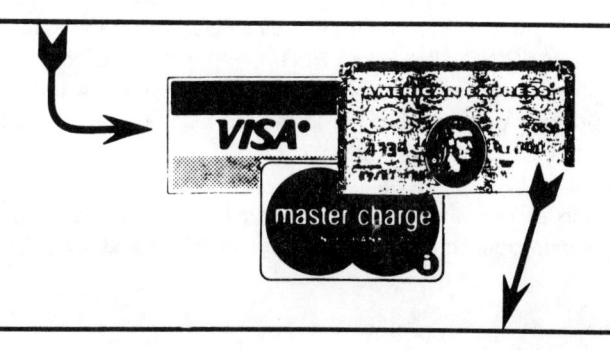

$50.00 per month repayment schedule of $500.00 debt at 18% Interest

	Loan Balance	Repayment	Interest Payment	Principal Reduction
1st month	$500.00	$50.00	$7.50	$42.50
2nd month	457.50	50.00	6.86	43.14
3rd month	414.36	50.00	6.22	43.78
4th month	370.58	50.00	5.56	44.44
5th month	326.14	50.00	4.89	45.11
6th month	281.03	50.00	4.22	45.78
7th month	235.25	50.00	3.53	46.47
8th month	188.78	50.00	2.83	47.17
9th month	141.61	50.00	2.12	47.88
10th month	93.73	50.00	1.41	48.59
11th month	45.14	45.82	.68	45.14
12th month	—0—			

Many taxpayers prefer to receive a tax refund because they know they lack the discipline to set aside and save money. For them, advance overpayment of taxes is a forced savings plan and the refund is their dividend.

If you have been in that category, the information in this book should enable you to change.

How Can I Reduce My Income Taxes?

This is a good question because, although you have a legal and patriotic obligation to pay your fair share of taxes, you also have a responsibility to yourself and your family to pay no more than is legally required of you. The basic answer to this how-to question is: education. There are numerous good books readily available on this subject; free literature is available from the IRS; magazines like MONEY, CHANGING TIMES and PERSONAL FINANCE continually report on tax reduction strategies; and, of course, the services of a good accountant who will not only prepare your tax forms but also advise you on tax matters are all very helpful.

Some things worth learning and inquiring about are tax-exempt or tax-deferred investments such as municipal bonds, IRA or Keough accounts and tax-deferred annuities.

What Is "Compound Interest"?

This question goes directly to the core of creating financial independence through savings and investments.

Compound Interest is interest earned and paid on a principal amount plus the interest it generates. The interest is paid on principal and interest, on top of interest, on top of interest.

For example, if one has $1,000.00 in the bank earnning 10 percent interest, at the end of the first year it would have earned $100.00. The new balance would be $1,100.00. At the same interest rate, the value at the end of the second year, due to compound interest, would be $1,210.00. The original $1,000.00 earned another $100.00 and the first year's earnings of $100.00 earned $10.00. The $10.00 represents interest on interest. It is money that was earned by money that one didn't have to work for to acquire.

(See Chart on next page)

$1,000.00 Investment Earning 10 Percent Compound Interest

	Value At Beginning Of Year	Profit (Interest)	Value At End Of Year
1st year	$1,000.00	$100.00	$1,100.00
2nd year	1,100.00	110.00	1,210.00
3rd year	1,210.00	121.00	1,331.00
4th year	1,331.00	133.00	1,464.00
5th year	1,461.00	146.00	1,610.00
6th year	1,611.00	166.00	1,772.00
7th year	1,772.00	177.00	1,949.00
8th year	1,949.00	195.00	2,144.00
9th year	2,144.00	214.00	2,358.00
10th year	2,358.00	236.00	2,594.00
15th year	3,797.00	380.00	4,177.00
20th year	6,116.00	612.00	6,728.00
25th year	9,850.00	985.00	10,835.00

(After ten years, the $1,000.00 investment has earned $1,594.00 profit. In 25 years, it has earned $9,835.00.)

To achieve the maximum return from compound interest, the interest profits must be tax-exempt or tax-deferred.

Tax-exempt means that the profits are not taxable income. Municipal bonds are an example of a tax-exempt investment.

Tax-deferred means that the profits accumulate without being taxed until the money is removed from the investment. Then it is taxed as income. IRA's, Keough plans and pension plans are tax-deferred investments.

$1,000.00 Investment At 10 Percent Rate Of Return

	Tax-Exempt	Tax-Deferred
Original Investment	$1,000.00	$1,000.00
Value After 10 Years	2,594.00	2,594.00
Taxes (At 25% Rate)	—0—	649.00
Value Of Investment After Taxes	2,594.00	1,945.00

An investment that is not tax-exempt nor tax-deferred increases in value at a slower rate as a portion of the profit must be paid in taxes each year. The rate of return is reduced by a percentage equal to the tax bracket of the taxpayer. For example, a 10 percent rate of return, for a taxpayer in the 25 percent tax bracket, becomes a 7.5 percent return (10% less 2.5%).

$1,000.00 Investment Earning A 10 Percent Profit For An Investor In The 25 Percent Tax Bracket

	Value At Beginning Of Year	Profit	Taxes (Minus)	Value At End Of Year
1st year	$1,000.00	$100.00	$ 25.00	$1,075.00
2nd year	1,075.00	108.00	27.00	1,156.00
3rd year	1,156.00	116.00	29.00	1,243.00
4th year	1,243.00	124.00	31.00	1,336.00
5th year	1,336.00	137.00	34.00	1,436.00
6th year	1,436.00	144.00	36.00	1,544.00
7th year	1,544.00	154.00	39.00	1,660.00
8th year	1,660.00	166.00	42.00	1,784.00
9th year	1,784.00	178.00	45.00	1,918.00
10th year	1,918.00	192.00	48.00	2,062.00
15th year	2,753.00	275.00	69.00	2,959.00
20th year	3,952.00	395.00	99.00	4,248.00
25th year	5,673.00	567.00	142.00	6,098.00

There are three factors that contribute to the accumulation of wealth with compound interest: first, the larger the initial investment, the greater the profit. This is quite obvious. This should not discourage you, though, from getting started saving and investing with small sums. Waiting until you have a large amount to invest is counter-productive.

Second, the larger periodic investment, the greater the profit. $100.00 added to your IRA account each month all year long is better than $1,200.00 put in all at once at the end of the year. Each of the periodic deposits begin earning interest from the date of deposit.

Third, the larger the rate of return, the greater the profit. Even 1%, even ½% difference in interest rates has importance over an extended period of time. It's generally true that the higher the rate of return, the greater the risk. This may not be true between banks and savings and loans with a 1% or 2% difference in interest rates between them. But, once you're out from under the Federal Government insurance of invested funds and into 10%+ annual returns, it is valid, and you have to balance concerns for growth of capital with safety of capital.

Time, as we've previously discussed, is a factor. The longer the uninterrupted term of the investment, the greater the profit. For that reason, your invested funds and the accumulating profits from compound interest should not be "robbed."

RULE OF 72

The **Rule of 72** is a useful aid to estimate how long it will take to double money, at various rates of return, with compound interest. Money **doubles** when the number of years the money is invested is multiplied by the rate of return equals 72. That is, $100.00 invested at 8 percent interest rate of return, will increase to approximately $200.00 in 9 years. Eight times 9 equals 72. At 6 percent rate of return, money doubles in 12 years. Six times 12 equals 72.

Original Investment	Rate Of Return	Term	Value
$1,000.00	5%	15 Years	$2,078.00
1,000.00	6%	12 Years	2,012.00
1,000.00	7%	10 Years	1,967.00
1,000.00	8%	9 Years	1,999.00
1,000.00	9%	8 Years	1,992.00
1,000.00	10%	7 Years	1,948.00
1,000.00	12%	6 Years	1,974.00
1,000.00	15%	5 Years	2,011.00
1,000.00	20%	4 Years	2,073.00

Should I Rent Or Buy A Home?

There are several factors that we must consider when answering that question. NEED is one of them. If you need more space, a home or even a condominium may be preferable to an apartment. LIFESTYLE is another factor. Some lifestyles are better matched to the minimal responsibilities of renting. And, even as a tenant, those responsibilities are usually less when renting an apartment than when renting a home. Others may have strong desires to decorate their living environment to their taste, want the freedom to remodel and modify as they see fit and be cheerfully willing to accept the responsibilities of maintenance, repair, upkeep, landscaping and gardening. Home ownership is their obvious choice.

The overriding control factor, though, is financial for most people. The availability of homes in a certain price range in your area can affect your decision. Current interest rates and financing options may affect your decision.

Historically, home ownership has proved to be a positive financial move for just about everybody and there is no reason to expect that to change much in the future, although there are a few areas in the country where real estate prices may have peaked. There is much talk, as this book is written, about the sudden, excessive inflation of home prices in Hawaii due to massive purchasing by the Japanese. With these very few and far between oddities aside, home ownership is a good investment for most people.

The following charts will help you evaluate the differences that develop for renters versus home owners:

ADVANTAGE COMPARISON

RENTING

1. The substantial investment of a down payment is not necessary.

2. It is much less complicated, less time-consuming and usually less expensive to relocate.

3. May allow metropolitan living and a decrease of commuting time and costs.

OWNING

1. Takes advantage of tax laws that permit the taxpayer to deduct mortgage interest payments and property taxes.

2. Creates equity accumulation as monthly mortgage payments gradually repay the loan.

3. If the house appreciates in value, the owner profits at the time of sale.

The following figures are based on owning with a $60,000.00 loan balance or renting a home of equivalent value.

STEP ONE: Determine out-of-pocket expenses.

	OWNING MONTHLY	OWNING ANNUALLY	RENTING MONTHLY	RENTING ANNUALLY
Rent	—0—	—0—	$800.00	$9,600.00
Mortgage Payment	$527.00	$6,319.00	—0—	—0—
Insurance (Homeowner's or Tenant's)*		400.00		100.00
Maintenance		500.00		—0—
Property Taxes		1,000.00		—0—
Annual Total		$8,219.00		$9,700.00

STEP TWO: Determine annual earnings on money invested rather than used as down payment, tax savings, principal accumulation and property appreciation.

	OWNING	RENTING
Profit from invested money not used for down payment and closing costs ($20,000.00 + $2,000.00 = $22,000.00 earning 7% = $1,54.00 — less taxes in 25% bracket = $1,155.00)	—0—	$1,155.00

Homeowner's Tax Deductions
   Interest $5,985.00
   Property Taxes 1,000.00
                    $6,985.00

Tax Savings (25% Bracket)	$1,746.00	—0—
Principal Accumulation	334.00	—0—
Property Appreciation (3%)	2,400.00	—0—
Annual Total	$4,480.00	$1,155.00

STEP THREE: Determine Actual Costs

	Owning	RENTING
Expenses	$8,219.00	$9,700.00
Financial Benefits	− 4,480.00	− 1,155.00
Total Annual Expenses	$3,739.00	$8,545.00
Monthly Expenses	312.00	712.00

* To complete the example, arbitrary amounts for nsurance, maintenence, property taxes and appreciation were selected. The amounts do vary considerably from community to community and from year to year.

— 47 —

Which Type Of Home Mortgage Is Best?

You can probably guess the beginning of the answer; different mortgages are right for different people. We live in a time of innovative and very competitive financing and, as a result, home loans are offered in a variety of formats and packages.

Remember, too, that lending institutions are businesses charged with making a profit. They essentially "rent" money at one rate and turn around and rent it out to others at a higher rate. The greater the difference in the rates, the greater their profit.

Your task is to obtain a home mortgage that is cost effective and otherwise effective for you. Since the selection will have long-term financial consequences, it must be made in a business-like manner.

There are four basic types of mortgages available to most people:

1. **FIXED RATE MORTGAGES.** The rate of interest and the monthly payment you pay remains the same for the entire term of the loan. In the early years of this mortgage, your payments are mostly taking care of the interest with only a very small portion of the payment reducing the principal balance. In later years, the opposite occurs with most of the payments reducing the principal. VA and FHA mortgages, incidentally, are fixed rate mortgages. The main benefit of a fixed rate mortgage is just that — the fixed rate. You know precisely what your monthly obligation is going to be throughout the entire term of the loan.

2. **SHORT-TERM MORTGAGES.** This is identical to the fixed rate mortgage but ony for a short term, typically three to five years. At that time, the loan balance must be paid in full or you must completely refinance your property.

3. **ADJUSTABLE RATE MORTGAGES.** This loan structure permits the lender to periodically adjust, increase or decrease, the interest rate. You are assuming the risk of an increasing rate in exchange for an initial rate of interest that is less than that available from a fixed rate mortgage. You will want to be certain you understand the conditions under which your lender can increase the rate.

4. **GRADUATED MORTGAGES.** These loans are structured with gradually increasing payments to match expected increased earnings of the borrower. This is a sound approach if you are on a "career path" with some reasonable predictability of raises and promotions.

Each of these mortgages requires a down-payment. Lenders will not finance 100% of the purchase price. They'll require you to pay a minimum of 5% to 25% of the purchase price while financing the balance. This is the lender's means of "hedging his bet" so that, in the event of your default and his foreclosure, he is likely to recover the loan balance. From your standpoint, it's important to realize that the larger the down payment, the smaller the loan amount and monthly payments.

The following two charts show your monthly payment varies with the interest rate and how the length of the mortgage determines the division of your payments between interest and principal.

Monthly Mortgage Payments Vary With The Interest Rate

Interest Rate	Monthly Payments*
8%	$440.26
9%	482.78
10%	526.55
11%	571.40
12%	617.70

*For a 30-year mortgage and a $60,000.00 loan balance.

The Shorter The Term Of The Mortgage The Greater Is The Principal Portion Of The Mortgage

	Loan Balance	Term Of Mortgage	Monthly Payment*	Interest Payment	Principal Payment
1st Month	$60,000.00	15 Years	$644.77	$500.00	$144.77
2nd Month	59,855.00	15 Years	644.77	498.79	145.98
3rd Month	59,709.00	15 Years	644.77	497.58	147.19
1st Month	$60,000.00	25 Years	$545.23	$500.00	$ 45.23
2nd Month	59,954.00	25 Years	545.23	499.62	45.61
3rd Month	59,909.00	25 Years	545.23	499.23	46.00
1st Month	$60,000.00	30 Years	$526.55	$500.00	$ 26.55
2nd Month	59,973.00	30 Years	526.55	499.78	26.77
3rd Month	59,947.00	30 Years	526.55	499.56	26.99

*At 10% rate of interest.

When purchasing a home, you will also encounter "closing costs." These include expenses for a survey to verify the property boundaries, an appraisal to verify value, a title policy to insure that title to the property is free of liens, assessments or conflicting claims and the lender's charge to initiate the mortgage — typically called "points" with a point equal to 1% of the loan amount. This process protects you and the lender. Occasionally, a seller will pay part or all of the closing costs but, most often, you, the buyer, pay these costs.

There are also "clauses" that may appear in mortgages. A common one, favoring the lender, is an escalator clause. This allows increases in interest when certain conditions occur. You must anticipate enforcement of such increases and prepare for increased payments. Another common clause, this one favoring you, the buyer, has to do with prepayment. Most lenders allow you to prematurely prepay a portion of the loan each year without penalty.

In purchasing your home, you may be getting a new mortgage in one of the formats discussed or you may be assuming an existing mortgage. Either way, the financial magnitude of your loan requires careful evaluation of the terms and, probably, "shopping" the alternatives available.

Thanks to Federal truth-in-lending laws, lending institutions are required to disclose all the terms of a mortgage on a certain form. This form itemizes all costs and is a useful aid in comparing mortgages.

How To Save Money On Your Home Mortgage

There is no other money tip that can save the average American homeowner more than the simple idea of prepaying the home mortgage.

In the first year, of a typical home mortgage, 95% of the monthly payments go to interest not reduction of the principal. Only 5% is applied to actually reducing your loan balance. Even by the 12th year, 90% of each payment is still going to interest.

By prepaying the mortgage, with even slightly larger monthly payments, the overpayment speeds up the reduction of your loan balance. And, since the interest is based on the existing loan balance, each subsequent monthly payment has a slightly lessened interest payment and a greater reduction of loan balance.

Prepaying a home mortgage with a loan balance of $60,000.00, by adding a $100.00 extra principal reduction payment each month, will save an astounding $68,790.73 in interest over the life of the mortgage! And, it will speed up the full payment of the 30-year mortgage by 14 years.

For most people, there is simply no better way to wisely invest an extra $100.00 a month!

How Much Life Insurance Should I Have?

The amount of life insurance coverage you need and will want to have will vary at different times in your life.

One good basic method of determining what your minimum coverage should be is evaluating the financial needs of your dependents if you should die. The sum of all debts, plus living and educational expenses for the years that your children, spouse and others are relying on your income, provides the total needed.

For example, if a family of four (father, mother and children, ages eight and ten) have a net income of $25,000.00 per year, that income or a percentage of it must be protected. If the income is solely from the father's salary, a life insurance on the father is indicated. Working with an accountant, an estimate of Social Security benefits and income from the mother's full or part-time employment can be totalled. Next, an estimate of living expenses until the chidren are 18 to 22 years old, depending on whether a college education is anticipated, can be calculated.

Example Of Family Budget

	With Father Living	If Father Dies
Father's Income	$ 25,000.00	—0—
Mother's Income (part-time)	—0—	$ 6,000.00
Social Security	—0—	8,000.00
Living Expenses	(23,000.00)	(19,000.00)
Excess/(Shortage)	2,000.00	(6,000.00)

In ten years, the youngest child will be 18 years old. There is a need for a minimum of $60,000.00 to take care of a $6,000.00 shortage each year. Since the purpose of life insurance is to provide needed funds if death should occur, the least expensive life insurance, that will provide this protection, should be purchased. If the existing family budget allows for more than the minimum protection, without altering the existing family lifestyle, additional protection should be considered. The aid of an accountant will help provide a more accurate estimate of the role of inflation, the benefits of Social Security and the taxes due on income.

What Type Of Life Insurance Should I Buy?

There may well be more different life insurance plans offered today than airline fares and schedules! It is way beyond the scope of our book to define and compare all these different plans. However, there are a few basic observations that will get you started in the right direction.

First, "term life" is a means of buying only protection. The other types of life insurance, including "whole life", "variable life", "universal life" and "endowment", combine protection with different types of savings plans.

There is great debate among personal finance experts on the pros and cons of savings via insurance versus savings through other means. Many financial planners stick to this simple device: insure with term, invest the rest elsewhere. Their advice is based on the fact that the rate of return on the savings portion of a life insurance policy is typically less than the rate of return available in other safe investments.

Under present tax laws, however, the profits (interest earned) that accumulate in the savings portion of life insurance policies have the advantage of being tax deferred. Also, some people find it much easier to save through life insurance than through other means.

What Other Types Of Insurance Should I know About?

Health insurance or medical insurance is offered as an employee benefit of most full-time jobs today. It is necessary to protect yourself from a financial wipeout caused by serious illness or injury. If not provided through your job, you should purchase such coverage for yourself.

Disability insurance provides a monthly benefit payment to you if you are unable to work for an extended period of time due to accidental injury or illness. This type of insurance provides funds to you, the disabled person, and your dependents. Unfortunately, the cost of this type of insurance is often rather high. Still, it's worth considering and investigating.

Annuities are unique insurance programs that can provide you with a monthly payment of pre-determined value for a certain number of years or for life. You can purchase annuities with a single lump sum payment or with a schedule of periodic payments.

The amount of the monthly check paid back to you through the annuity depends on the amount you invested, the period of time the insurance company had use of the money and your age when the benefit payments are scheduled to begin.

The annuity may be left to perform for you as scheduled or you may withdraw amounts of principal and interest, from time to time, or you may borrow against the value of the annuity. Different restrictions are built into different plans.

The main objective of an annuity is to protect you from out-living your other financial resources. Annuities are popular options for people who suddenly come into large sums of money through inheritance, the sale of a business or home or winning a sweepstakes, for example.

$10,000.00 Single-Premium Deferred Annuity versus $10,000.00 Investment

	Investment	Annuity
Amount Invested	$ 10,000.00	$ 10,000.00
Rate Of Return	12%	12%
Investment Term	20 Years	20 Years
Cumulative Annual Taxes Paid (25% Tax Bracket)	15,341.00	—0—
Value In 20 Years	56,044.00	96,463.00
Taxes Due At Withdrawal (25% Tax Bracket)	—0—	21,616.00
Value (After Taxes)	56,044.00	74,847.00
Less Original Investment	(10,000.00)	(10,000.00)
Profit	$ 46,044.00	64,487.00
Difference		+ $ 18,803.00

Is It Smart To Invest In Mutual Funds?

Many experts say that the only sensible way for "the small investor" to invest in the stock and money markets is through mutual funds. A mutual fund is a professionally managed group of investments. Individual investors then invest in shares in the fund. The fund's management receives a fee for administering the fund.

The idea is that by pooling their resources, many small investors in such a fund benefit from the same type of astute professional management as the large institutional investors do.

Other benefits are diversification within the funds, the ability to invest small amounts of money and liquidity.

If one stock owned by the fund performs poorly, the other stocks in the fund may still lead to overall satisfactory performance. Some funds permit investments of as little as $50.00; most accept investments of as little as $500.00. And, most funds permit the removal of the funds at any time or the switching of the invested funds from one fund to another managed by the same firm.

Is It Smart To Invest In An IRA?

An IRA is an Individual Retirement Account and a tax shelter that is legal, safe and available to all wage earners as well as most small businesspeople.

The two main reasons to invest in an IRA are:
1. Contributions may be 100% tax deductible whether you itemize deductions or not.
2. Taxes on IRA earnings are deferred, allowing your money to grow and multiply much faster than in taxable investments.

The Charts below show the growing values of IRA Accounts and the values of the tax savings provided by the IRA Accounts.

IRA Investment

Annual Contribution	$ 2,000.00	$ 2,250.00	$ 4,000.00
Rate Of Return	10%	10%	10%
Value At 10 Years	31,875.00	35,859.00	63,750.00
Value At 20 Years	114,550.00	128,869.00	229,100.00
Value At 30 Years	328,988.00	370,111.00	657,976.00
Value At 40 Years	885,185.00	995,833.00	1,770,370.00

(A $4,000.00 annual contribution earning 15% for 40 years would have a value of $7,116,361.00)

Value Of Invested Tax Savings

Annual IRA Contribution	$ 2,000.00	$ 2,250.00	$ 4,000.00
Tax Savings Invested Annually	500.00	563.00	1,000.00
Rate Of Return	10%	10%	10%
Tax (25% Tax Bracket)	(2.5%)	(2.5%)	(2.0%)
Net Rate Of Return	7.5%	7.5%	7.5%
Value Of Tax Savings At 10 Years	7,074.00	7,965.00	14,147.00
Value Of Tax Savings At 20 Years	21,652.00	24,381.00	43,304.00
Value Of Tax Savings At 30 Years	51,700.00	58,214.00	103,399.00
Value Of Tax Savings At 40 Years	113,628.00	127,945.00	227,256.00

(To evaluate the total value of an IRA investment, the value of the IRA and the value of the invested tax savings must be totalled.)

To maximize the benefits of an IRA, contributions should be initiated as soon as one is financially able to do so. Wise investors contribute as soon as possible after January 1st of each year. For example, an IRA contribution for 1989 should be made in January of 1989, even though it may be made any time until the 1989 tax return is filed.

**Comparison Of IRA Contributions On January 1st
And April 15th Of The Following Year**

	January 1st	April 15th Of Next Year
Annual Contribution	$ 2,000.00	$ 2,000.00
Rate Of Return	10%	10%
Value In 10 Years	31,875.00	25,866.00
Value In 20 Years	114,550.00	98,964.00
Value In 30 Years	328,988.00	288,564.00
Value In 40 Years	885,185.00	780,335.00

Also, to maximize the benefits of an IRA, you should make the allowable contribution. If your immediate needs limit the contribution, make as large a contribution as you can.

There is a 10 percent penalty for withdrawal of IRA funds prior to age 59½. If it is likely that the funds will be needed within seven years, the penalty may exceed the advantage over a non-IRA investment. That, however, will depend on the rate of return and the individual's tax bracket. Beyond seven years, the value of the IRA, less any withdrawal penalty, will usually exceed the value of a non-IRA investment.

Where Should I invest My IRA Funds?

In the beginning, the financial advantage of your IRA is from the tax savings and not from the yield on the investment. Since the invested amount is small compared to future years, the funds should be placed in an investment that will not incur a management fee that would reduce the amount of money available for investment.

As time goes on, your IRA funds can be invested in a broad range of investments. Some investments, such as a Certificate of Deposit or a money market account, are low risk and are guaranteed to preserve the invested capital. This type of account should be the choice of investors who are relying on their IRA funds for their retirement income.

If you are willing to take more risk, you can open an IRA account with a mutual fund. Many mutual funds allow you to move part or all of your investment to other funds in their family of funds. Within the family of funds, there may be a low risk money market fund as well as stock income and growth funds with more risk. Generally, the greater the profit potential on an investment, the greater is the risk of no profit or loss of investment capital. As a more adventurous investor, you can even invest in highly speculative investments which may bring tremendous profits or result in loss of all of the invested funds.

Since earnings in an IRA are tax deferred, there is no reason to invest IRA funds in municipal bonds or other tax-advantaged investments. For most IRA investors, the best investment will be the low risk investment with the highest yield. Over many years, even one percentage difference in rate of return can be substantial. For example, a 30-year-old couple that invests $4,000.00 per year, in an IRA that yields 10%, will have a nest egg of $1,084,098.00 when they are 65 years old. At an 11% yield, their nest egg would be $1,366,358.00. Just one percentage point increase in yield is worth an amazing $282,260.00.

What Is The Cost Of Not Having An IRA?

The higher your tax bracket, the greater the cost! If you have funds to invest in an IRA but choose not to do so, the decision will cost you several hundred thousand dollars (even if you invest the same $2,000.00 every year in a non-IRA investment). Annual profits on the non-IRA investment are subject to income taxes while the profits on an IRA investment are tax deferred.

Comparison Of A $2,000.00 Annual Non-IRA Investment With A $2,000.00 IRA Investment

	$2,000.00 Non-IRA Investment	$2,000.00 IRA Investment
Tax Bracket	25%	—0—
Rate Of Return	10%	10%
Value In 10 Years	$ 28,294.00	$ 31,875.00
Value In 20 Years	86,609.00	114,550.00
Value In 30 Years	206,799.00	328,988.00
Value In 40 Years	454,513.00	885,185.00

THE CURRENT RULES FOR IRA CONTRIBUTIONS

1. Up to $2,000.00 of a wage earner's income can be contributed.

2. Married couples can contribute up to $2,250.00 if one spouse has, at least, $2,000.00 earned income and the other has no income.

3. Married couples can contribute 100 percent of earned income, up to a maximum of $4,000.00, if each person has, at least, $2,000.00 of earned income.

4. Cash contributions for a year can be made from January 1st of that year until the tax return for that year is filed.

5. Cash contributions can be made up to age 70½.

6. Withdrawals are taxed as earned income and all the money must be removed by age 72.

7. A 10 percent penalty is paid on withdrawals prior to age 59½ except in cases of disability or death.

8. Taxpayers who are active participants in employer-sponsored retirement plans and Keough plans are not eligible for their IRA contribution unless their income is below $25,000.00 on a single taxpayer and below $40,000.00 on a joint return. The deduction is gradually eliminated as incomes increase to $35,000.00 and $50,000.00, respectively.

(IRA Rates may change. Consult your accountant.)

Are Keough And Pension Plans Useful To Me?

Much like an IRA, Keough and pension plans are designed to provide for a secure retirement. In all such plans, funds are invested and increase in value safe from taxes until they are withdrawn. Also, the funds invested in the plans may provide a tax deduction.

Pension plans are corporate retirement programs. A Keough Plan is a special retirement savings plan for self-employed individuals.

Employees of a corporation, or self-employed individuals, can look upon contributions to a retirement plan as an attractive benefit. Typically, the contribution to the plan on behalf of the employee does not result in a reduction of salary but is a benefit to salary.

Examples Of Retirement Fund Values

A self-employed individual, with an income of $50,000.00 per year, can make a $7,500.00 tax-deductible contribution to Keough Plan.

A corporate executive, with a $120,000.00 per year salary, may receive a pension benefit of $30,000.00 per year.

Year	Rate Of Return			Rate Of Return		
	5%	10%	15%	5%	10%	15%
1	$ 7,875	$ 8,250	$ 8,625	$ 31,500	$ 33,000	$ 34,500
2	16,143	17,325	18,544	64,575	69,300	74,175
3	24,826	27,308	29,950	99,304	109,230	119,801
4	33,942	38,288	43,068	135,769	199,820	172,271
5	43,514	50,367	58,153	174,057	201,468	232,612
10 6	99,050	131,484	175,120	396,204	525,935	700,478
20 7	260,394	475,519	883,576	1,041,577	1,890,075	3,534,304
30 8	523,206	1,357,076	3,749,677	2,092,823	5,428,303	14,998,708

Can You Explain
The "Economic Forces" That Affect Me?

Inflation is the main economic force that will affect every aspect of your finances throughout your entire life.

To understand inflation, you have to think about the purchasing power of the dollar. If it costs $2.00 to buy an item that previously sold for $1.00, the item is assumed to have increased or inflated in price. Actually, the item retained its original value and the purchasing power of the dollar decreased.

As with any commodity, the value of money is inversely proportional to its availability. In other words: the greater the supply, the less the value. When the government prints more dollars, and increases the money supply, each dollar becomes less valuable.

Inflation negatively affects your purchasing power. If or when you live on a fixed income, inflation really has a strong adverse effect. Many people who are fortunate to have steadily increasing incomes still never get increased purchasing power because of inflation.

An example of the effects and potential effects of inflation appears in the following chart.

To Maintain Purchasing Power

1970 Income	1980 Income	1990 Income
$ 5,000.00	$10,676.00	$ 25,697.00
10,000.00	22,552.00	55,941.00
20,000.00	46,744.00	118,689.00
30,000.00	73,171.00	177,405.00

(Source: U. S. News & World Report — July 14, 1980)

The above chart assumes wages from a single worker, deductions at the greater of 17% or the standard deduction, federal income and Social Security taxes paid and inflation in the 1980's identical to the 1970's.

Example Of Decreased Purchasing Power Of Money In A Savings Account Earning 7 Percent During A Period Of 10 Percent Inflation

	Account Value If Income Tax Is Paid From Account	Savings Account Value	Purchasing Power
Deposit	$1,000.00	$1,000.00	$1,000.00
After 1 Year	1,053.00	1,070.00	953.00
After 2 Years	1,108.00	1,145.00	907.00
After 3 Years	1,166.00	1,225.00	864.00
After 4 Years	1,227.00	1,311.00	823.00
After 5 Years	1,292.00	1,403.00	784.00
After 6 Years	1,359.00	1,501.00	747.00
After 7 Years	1,431.00	1,605.00	711.00
After 8 Years	1,506.00	1,718.00	678.00
After 9 Years	1,585.00	1,838.00	645.00
After 10 Years	1,668.00	1,967.00	615.00

In order for an investment to keep pace with inflation, after the income tax is paid, the investment return must exceed the rate of inflation by several percentage points. Unfortunately, increases in salary will result in increased federal, state and Social Security taxes. An income increase, resulting in a move to a higher tax bracket, could produce no financial benefit and could even result in financial loss.

Inflation **will** continue. It has been with us for decades, steadily eroding the value of the dollar. The purchasing power of the dollar has decreased to less than a dime since 1900. That means that today's dollar will buy an item that cost 10¢ in 1900. This is easily documented by following the price increases of a loaf of bread or a quart of milk.

The real cause of inflation is deficit spending by the Federal government. If the government spends more money than it takes in, the deficit is funded by increasing the national debt and the money supply. Both are inflationary. And, political posturing aside, deficit spending is very, very likely to continue for many years.

Inflation does help those who owe money. For example, if the Federal government pays off the national debt, it will be paid off with "cheaper" dollars, dollars that are worth less and easier to acquire.

During inflation, any loan (such as a home mortgage loan) is repaid with cheaper dollars. A salary increase provides more dollars to repay a fixed mortgage payment.

Inflation appears to increase the value of many things. For example, gold and silver coins and real estate appear to become more valuable during times of inflation. Actually, their value remains constant as the dollar decreases in value. Most homeowners realize that the value of their property increases each year in comparison to the dollar — due to inflation.

Inflation rewards the borrower and the owner of real estate and it is likely that it is here to stay. It is important to make it work for us and to know that it can.

If you become involved in your own business, awareness of the tax benefits tied to depreciation is extremely important. Business equipment costing $15,000.00 has a depreciation life of five years, for example, the business is eligible for a $3,000.00 tax deduction each year for five years. This type of deduction encourages the purchase of equipment and their depreciable assets which is viewed as a stimulus to the economy and creates more jobs.

And, everyone must understand both inflation and depreciation with the thought of acquiring things that appreciate (such as real estate) rather than things that depreciate.

Speaking Of Cars — Is It Better To Buy Or Lease?

The main advantages of leasing are:

1. Leasing requires only a small up-front payment, sometimes even no up-front payment. Not having to make a sizeable down-payment frees money for investment.

2. If you want to drive a new car every two to three years, leasing provides a more convenient way of exchanging the vehicles than selling or trading-in and buying each time. There are even lease plans that automatically provide for the exchange every so many years.

3. Leasing lets the lessor keep certain tax credits and depreciation, which reduces the amount of profit the lessor must make directly from your payments. That's why lease payments may be lower than purchase payments for the same car.

4. Leasing spreads out payment of sales taxes.

The main drawbacks of leasing are:

1. The contract will probably include penalties for premature termination. You lose the flexibility of escaping a monthly payment obligation, at any time, just by selling your car.

2. The lease contract may include mileage limits and extra charges for excess mileage.

3. The lack of a down payment may tempt you to commit to a car that is actually beyond your budget.

Should I Have A Will?

Only if you want to be the one deciding who receives your assets when you die. The lack of a will gives others this right! Your will should be prepared by an attorney who understands your financial position and your wishes. And, your will should be up-dated, periodically, as your finances change.

The Big Question: How Do I Become A Millionaire?

The number of millionaires grows considerably each year. One reason for the increase is that the deflated dollar makes accumulating a million of them easier! Still, unless you inherit or win a fortune, you'll probably find achieving a million dollar net worth difficult.

There are three basic categories of methods for achieving this lofty goal.

The first is through a talent or skill that commands a very high salary. Top-name entertainers and superstar athletes earn millions of dollars a year. Top college athletes often sign million dollar and multi-million dollar contracts on entry into the professional ranks. Surgeons, lawyers and highly skilled executives may earn salaries large enough to accumulate, through prudent investment, millionaire net worth.

The second approach is through business ventures. It is not at all uncommon for people who inherit family businesses or start their own to become wealthy. Typically, a great deal of work, sacrifice and risk is involved in the building of these fortunes.

The third approach is a combination of earning as much as possible, from your job or business, while keeping your standard of living quite low to permit maximum savings.

A common example of this approach is the many immigrants who came to the United States with little or no money, found jobs providing, at best, modest incomes but retained the standards of living they had known in their homelands, saved most of their earnings and accumulated wealth slowly and steadily over the years.

The bottom line of any of these approaches, though, is hard work to provide funds for investment and sensible financial planning.

* * * * * * * *

Whether you acquire a millionaire status or some lesser combination of financial security, a good quality of life and above-average earnings, the ideas we've discussed in this Chapter are extremely important. The more you know and understand about "money issues", the better you'll be able to make money work for you. For that reason, this Chapter and this book should not be viewed as an end-all of your personal financial education; instead, it's our hope that it will motivate you to continue investigating and learning more!

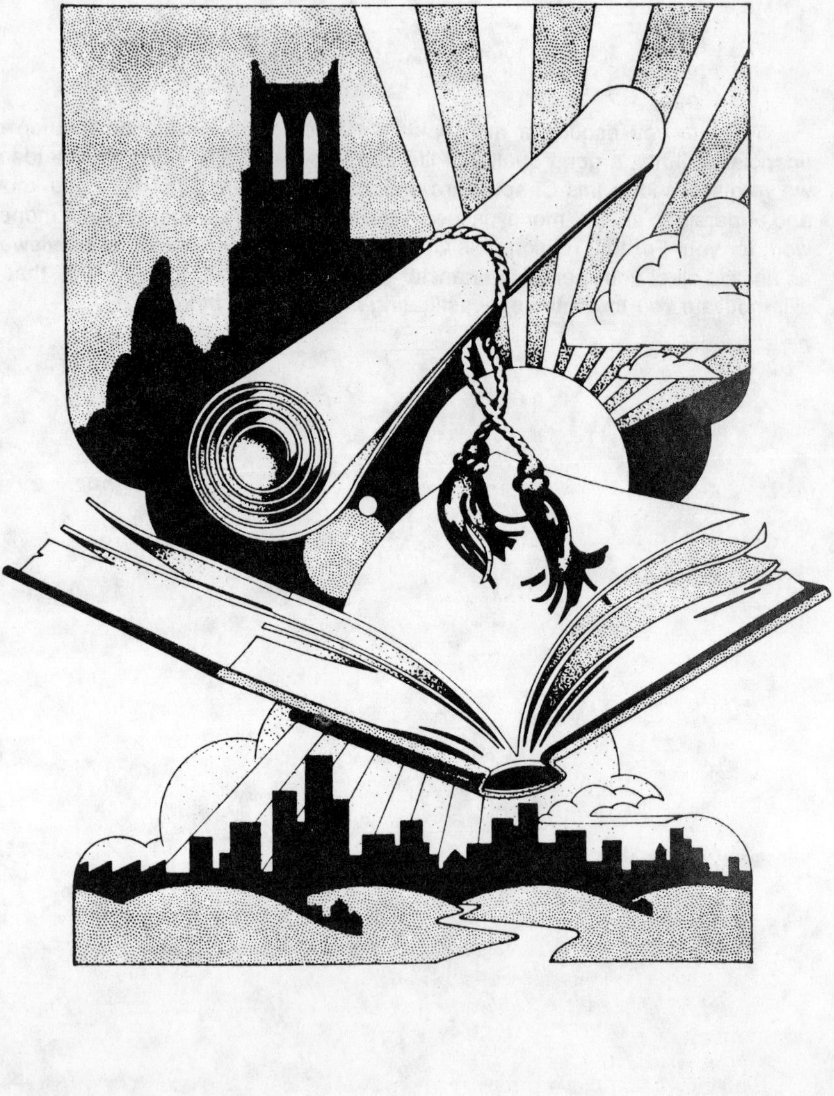

Chapter 10
THE ROLE OF EDUCATION

Education is big business. Educational institutions collect hundreds of millions, maybe billions, of dollars in tuition payments. Various courses and training programs are provided by many businesses as profit-making ventures.

You can improve your income and opportunities for advancement substantially with formal education and college degrees as well as completion of many privately offered seminars and courses.

College graduates earn an average of $600,000.00 more than non-graduates in 40 working years!

The objectives to keep in mind are the same whether you get education through formal, institutional channels; through independent study of books, tapes and lectures; or, through 'the school of experience'.

1. **Acquisition of knowledge.** The human mind can accumulate an immeasurable quantity of information even though much of what has been learned is forgotten. However, what we learn is often not as important as what we become capable of learning because of that which we have learned previously. For example, the study of early European history, although most may be forgotten, may permit a better understanding of European history thereafter. Similarly, basic mathematic exercises form the intellectual foundation for more advanced mathematic concepts.

Obviously, some knowledge has more practical value than others. That is, it is a prerequisite for acceptance into another course or profession. For example, to become an accountant, you must complete a particular curriculum to demonstrate that you have acquired certain knowledge. But, much of the knowledge is of little practical value. Its true value will be discussed later.

2. **Acquisition of Skills.** The more difficult that it is to achieve something, the more valuable that accomplishment is. That is, the greater the difficulty, the greater the glory! The many skills that we learn in our education system vary from the "basics", such as reading and listening, to the advanced skills in the sciences and medicine.

Through an education, we acquire new skills and learn to improve them. Having achieved a predetermined skill level, we become capable of and eligible to pursue increasingly more difficult skill levels. In time, we become a highly skilled individual capable of performing tasks that only those similarly trained can perform.

Education also plays a role in the maintenance of previously learned skills and knowledge. Continuing education and refresher courses rekindle the desire to retain knowledge and skills that may otherwise be lost. These courses also introduce new material, in accordance with the principle that **the mind must be challenged, and its knowledge increased, or its ability diminishes.**

The most important skills learned through an education are not measured; graded or tested. These are the personal development skills such as:

    1. the ability to listen and observe skillfully.

    2. learning to organize thoughts and manage time.

    3. selecting a personal achievement level.

    4. developing disciplined work habits.

    5. being responsible.

Educators seldom address the importance of developing these personal skills which may be much more important than grades.

Our attempt to acquire skills usually helps us to determine what are our talents. We must learn these essential skills on our own. Identifying our talents and developing them can provide a more satisfying and rewarding life.

3. **To alter life's direction.** Life is a journey. You make choices which determine your path for the journey. Some people do not believe this. They believe that they are unable to choose their path. As a result, they travel only the most popular route, with the masses, avoiding the slightly uphill and rocky path to a more rewarding life. They are surrounded by mediocrity.

Education enlightens the true student, providing information that increases his career and other life choices. It allows him to share his ideas with other educated people who also have high ideals and goals. We all tend to be like the people with whom we associate. They influence us and we influence them. **The influence that others have on us can play a significant part in the direction that our journey through life takes.** Therefore, choosing successful people as friends gives us a better opportunity to be successful. The combination of more knowledge and the positive influence of the people we associate with enhances life.

We believe education is the most valuable investment that you can make. It leads to career opportunities, self-confidence and greater income. While it does not guarantee financial success, it does insure greater opportunities which inevitably lead to a more satisfying and productive life. Finally, an education gives a person a better perspective on life, much like the view on a mountain peak differs from the view in the forest below.

Chapter 11
LEARNING TO LEARN

Possibly the most important statement made in this book is this: More than any other one thing in life, your ability to use your mental powers to learn and to think shapes your destiny!

If you are curious and continually searching for knowledge, if you have a strong desire for exceptional success, if you want a happy life, you will learn to study.

Educators have difficulty agreeing on what "learning" is. One thing we do know is that learning is an active process. Society in general and any profession or business in specific is changing too quickly to allow learning to be separate from living. The person who sighs with relief on graduation from school, thinking that the work of learning is behind him, is doomed to only 'average', at best, in his future.

Learning is better viewed as the process of reaching our potential. We never get there because potential grows with experience! That makes learning a lifelong self-improvement process.

Unfortunately, many people have only learned how to be taught but have not learned how to learn!

When you learn to make learning an active, enjoyable process, many things change. You can read faster with better comprehension. Be better prepared for formal educational programs, get more out of them and be confident and relaxed before and during exams. Be able to better concentrate and block distractions.

Here are some specific, very effective methods for learning from structured educational programs. If you are a high school or college student, these techniques will directly apply to you. If not, they can still help you better benefit from seminars, conferences and self-directed study. And, this information should also be passed on to your family members and friends who are high school and college students.

TECHNIQUES OF STUDY

Class Preparation: An instructor, who is interested in maximizing classroom learning, will encourage his students to prepare for each class by providing a schedule of topics to be covered in class and a coinciding list of preparatory reading. A prepared student then receives additional information on the topic during the lecture class rather than being introduced to new material. Taking notes becomes easier and understanding and comprehension is increased because the student is already somewhat familiar with the presented material. Because the subject matter is not new, intelligent questions can be asked during class.

Students who routinely prepare for class discover these benefits:
1. Classroom time is more enjoyable as understanding the presented material is easier (even if the instructor seems to ramble aimlessly).
2. Note taking is easier and more organized.
3. Less time is needed to study and learn the material after class as classroom time served as the first review.
4. Other students regard them as better students.
5. Their self-image improves.

In the Classroom: A student who misses classes creates a tremendous burden for himself. He fails to learn from class preparation, is usually without direct access to the material presented in class, does not have personalized notes and is destined to learn less and earn lower grades. **Students who are serious about their education do not "cut" classes.** They are eager to learn and consider attending class to be an important part of their opportunity for a better future.

Generally, the first and last five minutes of each class are the most important. In the first few minutes, the instructor usually reviews the material from the previous class and previews the material to be covered that day. This provides an opportunity for the student to review and to plan an outline for the new material.

Being in class is not enough. **To learn, a student must actively listen.** This may be difficult to master as most people have already trained themselves to block out certain sounds, such as the radio, television or conversations, as they think of something else. Blocking out the words of an instructor, who is a poor speaker presenting an uninteresting topic, may be all too easy. In addition, our ability to listen and think at a rate that is four times the rate that a lecturer provides information allows plenty of time for daydreaming.

To insure active listening and to retain important information from lectures it is necessary to take notes. **Effective note taking is a skill that must be developed.** Students must constantly strive to select only the important information to include in their notes to avoid volumes of notes. Better teachers will help their students determine what information should be recorded.

The following tips will help to insure good notes:
1. Use a separate spiral bound notebook for each subject. Write only on the left page. Leave the right page blank.
2. Date each lecture. Note the names of guest lecturers.
3. Learn to record approximately 20 percent of what is said in class. Students who take too many notes do poorly on tests.
4. Take organized notes using an outline format when possible. Keep the notes simple. Avoid crowding.
5. Use diagrams.
6. Learn speedwriting: a minimum number of words, abbreviations and symbols. For example, = for **equal**, # for **number**, w/ for **with**, w/o for **without**, etc.
7. Review library books on studying and taking of notes.

Importance of Scheduling: Students who do not prepare for classes are far behind those students who do prepare. The prepared student is familiar with the lecture material prior to class, uses class time as a learning and review session, takes better notes and understands the lecture more easily. The student who does not prepare is burdened with new information which must be learned after class.

Typically, the student who does not prepare for classes has a more difficult time preparing for exams. As a result, the life of the unprepared student is difficult, tense and unproductive.

Observing the planning and organization of some students quickly reveals that their studies are not a priority. They do not prepare for classes and often cut class. Their notes are poor and incomplete. Their study habits are ineffective and their grades are poor. These students are in a hopeless situation and are preparing themselves for a future of mediocrity unless they establish more important priorities in their lives.

The best method of developing a productive daily schedule is to:
1. **List** the activities that are planned for each day.
2. **Rank** each activity according to importance.
3. **Enter** each activity on a daily schedule. (Unscheduled hours are free time.)

In order for a schedule to be practical and productive, certain rules must be followed:
1. Never let a lower priority activity replace a higher priority activity. For example, do not agree to work at a job during class time.
2. Learn to keep to the schedule but have some flexibility. For example, free time may be interchanged with study time providing that study time is not decreased.
3. Do not allow others to alter the schedule.
4. Use free time as a reward for productive study time. Include sufficient rest, entertainment and aerobic exercise.

It is important to recognize that a schedule is necessary if we are committed to achieving certain objectives. Some people may consider a strict daily schedule to be too restrictive. They are wrong! Scheduling is not only necessary, for optimal productivity, it is a time saver, freeing time for discretionary activities. In addition, it ensures freedom from the guilt of not devoting sufficient time to studying. The habit of planning and adhering to a schedule when I was a student has continued to be a part of my life. I estimate that my productivity, because of planning and scheduling, is nearly double of what it would be without it.

The discipline that one develops by voluntarily adhering to what he expects of himself, via a daily schedule, will prove to be a very valuable asset in controlling his future. **Scheduling our activities gives us a big advantage over taking things as they come.** By making it more difficult to avoid a task, because it is written down, we ensure productivity.

(Continued on page 72)

Making good *Life Choices* has enabled Rich and Dawn to enjoy travel to seven European countries, Hawaii and the Bahamas plus ski trips, cruises and much more.

THE RIGHT MONEY CHOICES LEAD TO FINANCIAL SECURITY *AND* AN EXCITING LIFESTYLE!

Dawn Bence with daughter, Jamie, in front of the lakefront home.

THERE ARE MANY TIME CHOICES TO BE MADE ....

Richard's commitment to efficient time management has permitted a three-day workweek for the past eleven years.

Review Class Notes: To learn new material, it is important to understand it and review it several times. The less time there is between reviews, the less chance there will be to forget what was learned. It is important to review class notes, as soon after class as possible, while the information is still fresh in our minds.

A very effective way to review class notes is to rewrite them. If notes taken in class were written on the left page of a spiral bound notebook, the rewritten notes can be entered on the right page. To create notes which are easy to review, and suitable for self-quizzing, the following suggestions should be helpful.

1. Draw a vertical line, 2½" from the spiral, down the length of the right page.

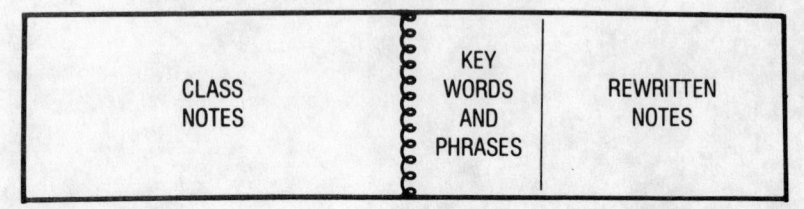

CLASS NOTES	KEY WORDS AND PHRASES	REWRITTEN NOTES

2. Using abbreviations, symbols, diagrams, etc., rewrite class notes in a legible and organized manner. Keep the notes brief.
3. In the left margin, write key words and phrases that correspond to the notes.

Rewriting class notes is an effective method of reviewing and learning the material presented in class. The immediate review helps to "fix" knowledge in our minds. **If that which is learned is not reviewed, it is soon forgotten and must be re-learned** in order to pass the course. The process of learning, unlearning and re-learning is all too familiar to students who do not periodically review what they have learned.

Having organized rewritten notes suitable for periodic review in preparation for examinations will substantially decrease the total time needed to learn the material. In addition, rewritten notes will be more legible and more organized than notes taken in class and easier to review in preparation for the next class or exam.

Assignments: One can race through written homework, in an effort to finish it as quickly as possible, or use it as the learning tool that it is intended to be. Solving math and science problems will help develop the skills necessary to pass the course. Copying someone else's completed homework is a waste of time, although it may solve the personal dilemma of the disorganized, unprepared, struggling student.

Language and social studies homework is just as valuable to learning. Doing it carefully helps to review words and concepts learned and promotes a better understanding of the subject material.

Reading assignments can be extremely time consuming for students, par-

ticularly for the untrained reader. Many college students are overwhelmed by the amount of reading that is assigned. The following suggestions will help to reduce the time devoted to reading and improve comprehension.
1. If you are untrained in effective reading methods, **acquire reading ability** through reading courses or from texts on the subject. Most methods taught will increase reading speed and comprehension.
2. Prior to reading a chapter, **skim** the bold type headings, tables, charts and pictures. Read the first and last three paragraphs of the chapter to identify the author's objective.
3. **Analyze your objective** for reading the material. Skim the chapter if you are merely looking for certain information. Read more thoroughly for assignments, adjusting your reading rate to the difficulty of the material.
4. **Be an active reader.** Note the important facts with a see-through marker, with notes in the margin or by taking notes while reading. It is better to read the paragraph once and then go back and make notes.
5. If the assigned reading or chapter is unusually long, divide it into parts that can be read at one sitting.
6. Avoid reading when fatigued or experiencing emotional problems.

Studying: Most students waste a lot of time while studying. It is not that studying is a waste of time but, rather, that their study methods are ineffective. As a result, they dislike studying because it is boring, time consuming and unproductive. The only way to make studying enjoyable is to make it effective, efficient and interesting.

To be effective, studying must result in learning the subject matter and achieving good test scores. **To be efficient**, studying must require no more than minimum time to learn the material. **To be interesting**, it must minimize boredom and lead to our ultimate objective, that is, course completion, a high grade and progress toward our educational goals. It must also eliminate relearning information that was learned but forgotten.

Effective studying depends on the quality of study time, not on its quantity. In fact, ineffective study, no matter how long one pursues it, won't help learning. And, in the long run, it could be a major factor in poor grades and the dropout rate. Spending the minimum time studying, while using effective study techniques is not only to be encouraged but is a necessity at higher levels of education.

The first consideration for effective study is to have a designated place to study. It can be any place that has a chair and desk, is free of clutter and has adequate light and ventilation. It must be free from interruptions of noise and people. Using the same place to study will soon result in a conditioned response to be able to concentrate when there.

Studying should be scheduled at a time when it is easiest to concentrate. Some people are more alert in the morning while others study better late in the day. For maximum effectiveness, we must understand our "alertness cycle" and capitalize on it by scheduling study time at that time each day.

Very few people can maintain a high level of concentration for more than an hour. Therefore, lengthy study sessions should have short breaks each hour. Assignments and reviews, if lengthy, should be divided into segments. This is known as studying in "units" by identifying and completing a series of sub-goals.

The person who studies effectively:
1. realizes that study begins when the course begins. It is not merely a pre-examination activity.
2. knows that study is divided into two parts. The **first** part is learning the material in class and from assignments. The **second** part is remembering what is learned. Researchers have demonstrated that we quickly forget much of what we have learned and, eventually, forget most of it. To prevent forgetting, the good student reviews the material as soon after learning it as possible and then reviews it often. At first, it may appear to be rather time consuming to be continually reviewing notes but it requires less time than re-learning that which was forgotten. **Ten minutes of review will offset one hour of re-learning.** Reviewing regularly requires discipline but it eliminates forgetting and saves time.
3. understands the material in his notes. He realizes that it is a worthless exercise to review something he does not understand. He seeks the help of instructors, the textbook and other students immediately if he does not understand something.
4. makes studying interesting by making it a challenge. He has goals and sets time limits.
5. attempts to remain worry-free so that optimal concentration is possible.
6. does the more difficult assignments first. An exception would be to complete several shorter assignments to direct all of his attention to a single, longer assignment.
7. learns effective study techniques. He carefully separates the material on his notes that need review from learned material, so that future reviews only include unlearned material. This can be accomplished by underlining the unlearned material, highlighting it with a see-through marker or identifying it by placing a dot in the margin next to it. As learning progresses, the quantity of material to be learned decreases with each review. During each subsequent review session, a different color marking can be used to identify unlearned material. This technique of compressing notes is so effffective that, as exam time approaches, less and less time is needed for review and no time is needed to re-learn forgotten information. In addition, it relieves the boredom of reviewing what has already been learned.
8. uses completion rewards as an incentive to make regular effective study a priority. This type of positive reinforcement following achievement is helpful and easy to implement. Effective studying frees time for other things that one enjoys doing. Predetermining a reward becomes a motivating factor to work hard at concentrating and completing the assignment in the specified time. In this way, planning leisure activities becomes an asset to studying rather than a liability.

Exam Preparation: The student who has prepared for classes, rewritten his notes and reviewed them regularly does not need to do a great deal of preparation for examinations. In fact, good students usually look forward to exams as a completion of a portion or semester of learning and an opportunity to show what they have learned.

Approximately three weeks prior to an exam a pre-examination review schedule should be established. Usually, five or six reviews of the subject matter will insure adequate preparation. Using the previously described technique of consolidating notes will decrease the time needed for each review. (Students without the benefit of good study habits will be increasing their exam preparation time as the exam date approaches. Often they run out of time.)

There are several things besides reviewing notes that a student can do to help prepare for an exam.
1. Make "flash cards": index cards with exam questions on one side and answers on the other side can aid in reviewing. The cards can be used to take advantage of short study times available while waiting five minutes for an appointment or on a fifteen-minute bus ride. When the information on a card is known, the card can be retired. As exam time approaches, there will be only a few cards left to review!
2. If "old tests" are available, review them. Often similar or identical questions will appear on the new test. Also, reviewing old tests is a good method of self-testing that familiarizes the student with the exam layout and eliminates surprises.
3. If the examination involves solving problems, as in chemistry or mathematics, time must be devoted to practicing problem-solving. The practice sessions should increase problem-solving speed and accuracy as well as self-confidence.
4. Reviewing for an examination with other prepared students may help to clarify terms or concepts and aid in problem-solving. Avoid preparing for exams with disorganized students who have nothing to offer a good student.

No discussion of preparing for exams would be complete without at least mentioning "cramming." Cramming is the last minute attempt to acquire the knowledge that is necessary to pass an examination. It is a risky way to try and get good grades as anxiety and panic often prevents retention of facts during the exam. It is a wasteful way to master knowledge, counterproductive to obtaining an education and an identifying attribute of poor students.

Exams and Grades: We are faced with examinations throughout our lives. They are part of personal improvement and career advancement. We are continually required to prove that we have become more knowledgeable and more competent by passing examinations.

For educational institutions, exams are necessary to verify that the student knows the course material. Some students will try to beat the system by taking the exam without knowing the material. They may "cram" or "cheat." Their participation in the educational system is developing negative personal traits. They become the **losers** that we described in Chapter One.

At some time in everyone's life, they are told that grades are not important. It is the acquired knowledge that advice is wrong **and** right.

It is **wrong** because grades are important. Ask any student receiving a "D" if the low grade he received is important. Then, ask the student receiving the "A" if the grade is important. Their answers will clarify any misconception on the importance of grades.

The advice is **correct** in stating that acquiring knowledge is important. It would be more meaningful and useful to advise students to acquire a good education and let their grades reflect their ability.

Good grades are important for two reasons:
1. They are a rough measure of a student's educational progress. And, admission into graduate and professional schools require good college grades.
2. Frequently, grades are a basis for one's estimation of self-worth. Our grades rank us among other students. They let us know how we have performed and give indicators of future performance. We may find ourselves basing our goals and aspirations on our grades.

To get good exam scores, we must be prepared for the exam. Would you agree that taking exams would be easy if you prepared for classes, took good notes and learned in class, improved class notes by rewriting them and reviewed those notes regularly? For the prepared student, exams are a chance for him to show what he knows. Fear of a poor grade is not a concern. In fact, most people are relaxed and confident taking exams if they have prepared. The prepared student has already passed the exam. His performance will determine if he gets an "A" or a "B."

Part of exam preparation is getting enough sleep the night before the exam. This should be preceded by a couple of hours of reviewing and some relaxing activity.

Observing the following suggestions should eliminate some errors that could lower a test score.
1. Use a checklist to verify that everything needed to take the test is available (including pencils, paper, watch, calculator, etc.)
2. Listen to and read instructions carefully. Ask for clarifications if necessary.
3. Learn how the exam will be graded. Is there a penalty for guessing?
4. Skim the exam. Complete the easier parts first.
5. Work at a pace that will insure completing the exam.
6. Read each question twice to be sure that you read it correctly. Re-phrase the question, if necessary. Notice critical or key words.
7. Mark difficult or unsure answers. If time permits, re-read the questions and check the answers.

Blocks to Learning: By employing the study habits described in this Chapter, there will be few blocks to learning. However, there are certain pitfalls that even the most conscientious student must be aware of:
1. **Poor scheduling.** A daily and weekly schedule is necessary to plan one's life.

Being too lazy or too busy to plan each day is symptomatic of a lack of dedication or a half-herated effort to achieve one's goals.
2. **Letting non-academic activities interfere** with studying is a problem for most students. Study is work and most other activities are fun. Self-discipline is necesary.
3. **Negative influences.** Anything that interferes with effective studying is a negative influence. Good students learn to minimize time spent with people who do not encourage and respect their good study habits. Negative influences can also come form one's self after failures. But these can be overcome by reviewing one's intense desire to achieve his goals.
4. **Alibis.** People who choose not to accept responsibility for their lives make excuses for their inadequacies. Habitually making alibis insures failure.

Lack of intelligence is the least likely reason for poor grades. Poor grades go hand-in-hand with poor study methods. To become an exceptional student, and to improve grades, we must do what the experts do. They set an exact goal, develop a plan to achieve it, maintain their enthusiasm and take positive action. Their consistent effort produces results that bolster their self-confidence and keep them on the path of success.

It is not necessary to write-off a desired career because you do not know how to study well. Implement the study methods in this Chapter and your academic accomplishments will improve. **Learn to be a good student.** By the way, those who study effectively are respected by others and their discipline is envied by other less-disciplined students.

You can be a success. You have all the ability that you need. Develop good study habits and accept your successes.

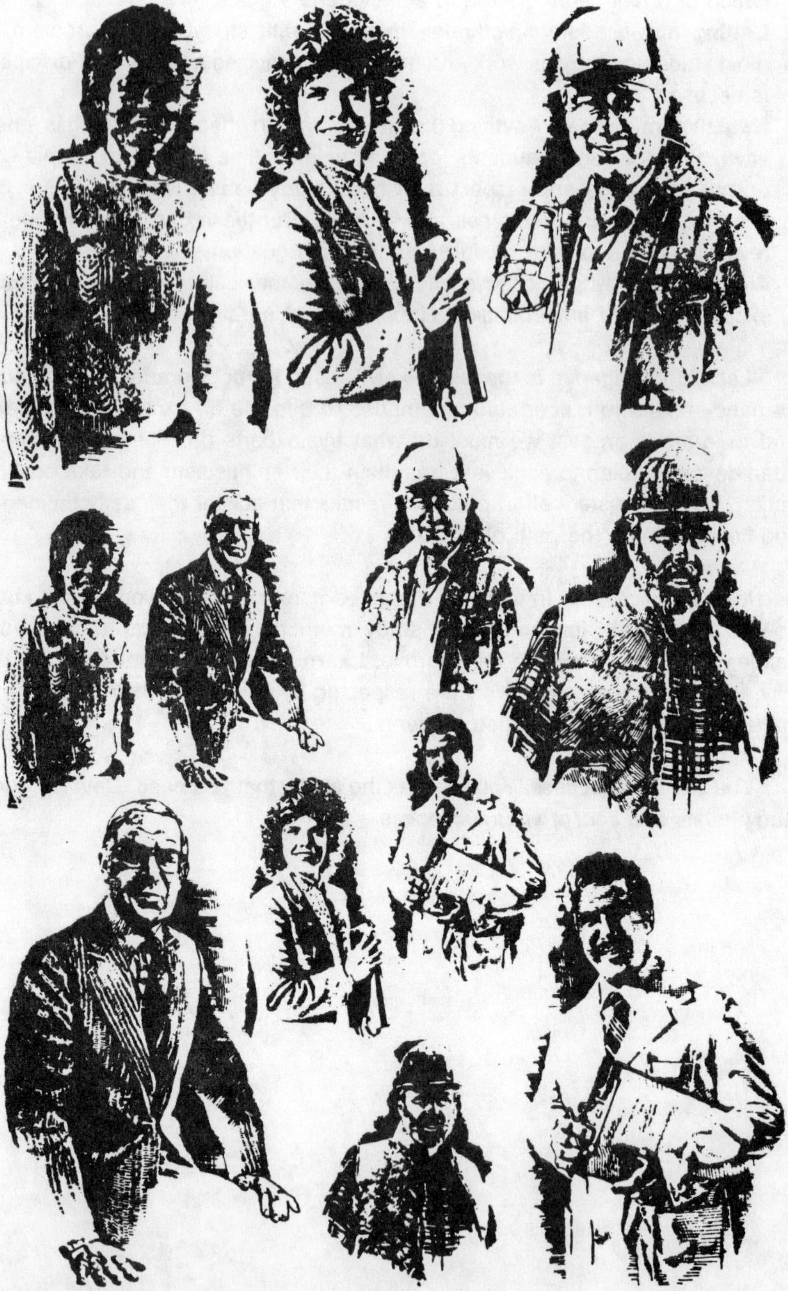

Chapter 12
CAREER CHOICES

Most people find choosing a career to be a very difficult task. The difficulty of the task causes many people to postpone it indefinitely. It is often, ultimately, replaced by taking the best of whatever comes along. As a result, many people wind up stuck in jobs not really suited to their interests and abilities. Gradually, they come to dislike this work. Frustration, resentment, self-pity and other negative emotions set in.

Obviously, you want to avoid this trap or, if already a victim to it, find a way to break free.

Why Are Career Choices So Difficult?

Many people intensify the difficulty by failing to get the information necessary for quality decisions!

There are many factors to be analyzed and considered in choosing a career and a great deal of solid information is needed to facilitate that analysis.

Today, you have a wider range of career options and possibilities than ever before!

Opportunities are everywhere! The best are available, of course, to the most competent individuals with the best education, personality traits and work habits.

As our careers progress, both fewer and better options become available. Fewer because we become more experienced, even specialized in a certain career field. And, as we advance in the corporate structure, there are fewer and fewer openings at the peak of the pyramid. But, better options also arise as we develop and demonstrate more ability.

With age, the number of career options decrease. They don't disappear but they do decrease. It's best to investigate career opportunities and make good decisions as early in life as possible.

3 Keys To Good Career Choices

1. GET TO KNOW YOURSELF. You **are** unique! No matter how much your talents or interests may resemble others, there is no one precisely like you. The more you know about you, the better your career choices can be.

Consider the best accomplishments in your life so far, the activities you like and dislike, your preferences for leadership responsibility versus teamwork and your best skills. Use these as clues to identifying career choices that "fit."

There's also value in discussing your self-assessment, and your career interests, with one or more persons you respect and trust.

Competent career counselors can also direct you to aptitude tests and interest inventories that help point out your interests and talents. These test results cannot tell you what to do but they will increase your self-awareness.

2. ANALYZE CAREER OPTIONS. Textbooks and magazines with "career lists" can be reviewed. Discussions with career counselors, placement professionals and people already employed in the fields that interest you can all be helpful. It's important to consider not just the present but also to look ahead a few years to evaluate the future.

3. MOVE IN THE RIGHT DIRECTION. You may not be able to take a direct route to your goals. But, if you constantly move in the direction of your goals, you will ultimately get there!

Even if you cannot see a final, ultimate, chief goal, you know what direction it must be in. Moving in that positive direction will provide you with relevant experience and information. You must not procrastinate just because you cannot clearly define the ultimate goal.

A suitable career direction must involve you in work you enjoy doing and must provide you with sufficient income to provide the lifestyle and security you strongly desire. You cannot overlook the issue of money when choosing a career.

If a lot of money and security, prestige and status are not particularly important to you, then you can choose a career that may only provide a basic standard of living although great personal satisfaction. If you want a high income, though, you have to select a career that pays well and that you can enjoy. If a conflict exists, you've got to carefully compromise or keep searching for the career that meets both monetary and fulfillment needs.

A Career Choice Is Not A "Life Sentence"

You should give great care to your career choice but, on the other hand, you need not allow it to create terrible fear or anxiety. Just as you have the freedom to choose one career, you have the freedom to change at, virtually, any time. Although there may be short-term negative consequences accompanying such a change, the long-term, overall benefits often outweigh them.

Today, it is common for a person to have two, or even three, careers in a working lifetime. Many people also have two simultaneous careers. These things will probably grow even more commmon as life expectancy increases.

We hope you'll look at your present and future career choices as challenging but positive and exciting opportunities.

AUTHORS' AFTERWORD

This book has been about the important choices we make in our lives. Every day we make many choices. Maybe even hundreds. Many are automatic. Easy. Habitual — like choosing to put the right shoe on before the left.

Many choices, though, have far-reaching consequences. Good choices nearly always work together to create a good life, a good career, a good future.

To make good choices, you have to believe in yourself and your ability to exercise great control over your life.

From time to time, you may be discouraged by certain experiences or by others. Being able to see past temporary discouragement is important. Walt Disney overcame the discouragement of being fired because he lacked good ideas. Beethoven persisted even after being judged "hopeless as a composer" by his music teacher. The list of examples could fill a book. You, too, most assuredly, have the ability to overcome any discouragements you may encounter and reach, virtually, any goals that are really important.

Our purpose in writing this book was to provide you with two things. First, we wanted to motivate you to pursue exciting, positive, rewarding goals in your life. Second, we wanted to give you information you need to make your progress easier, quicker and more certain.

You will grow or stagnate, become happier or stagnate. The choices are yours.

I bargained with life for a penny

And life would pay no more.

However I begged at evening

When I counted my scanty store.

For life is a just employer

Who gives you what you ask.

But, once you have set the wages,

Then you must bear the task.

I worked for a menial's hire

Only to learn dismayed

That any wage I had asked of life,

Life would have willingly paid.

— *Jesse B Rittenhouse*

If you think you are beaten — you are.
If you think you dare not — you don't.
If you'd like to win, but you think you can't,
It's almost a cinch that you won't.

If you think you'll lose — you've lost,
For out in the world you'll find
Success begins with a fellow's will,
It's all in the state of mind.

If you think you're outclassed — you are.
You've got to think high to rise.
You've got to be sure of yourself before
You can ever win a prize.

Life's battle doesn't always go
To the swifter or faster man,
But sooner or later the man who wins
Is the man who thinks he can.

— *from* **Think and Grow Rich**

"If you treat an individual as he is, he will stay as he is; but if you treat him as if he were what he ought to be and could be, he will become what he ought to be and could be."
— *Johann Wolfgang von Goethe*

"Keep away from people who try to belittle your ambitions. Small people always do that, but the really great make you feel that you, too, can become great."
— *Mark Twain*

Definition of a genius: a person who aims at something no one else can see and hits it.

"Genius is the power of lighting one's own fire."
— *John Foster*

"Genius is the only power to make continuous effort."
— *Elbert Hubbard*

"Just as the twig is bent the tree's inclined."
— *Pope*

"People are always blaming their circumstances for what they are. I don't believe in circumstances. The people who get on in this world are the people who get up and look for the circumstances they want and, if they can't find them, make them."
— *George Bernard Shaw*

"The opportunity isn't as rare as the ability to find it."
— *Jack Howell, Jr.*

"The optimist proclaims that we live in the best of all possible worlds; the pessimist fears this is true."
— *James Branch Cabell*

"The mass of men live lives of quiet desperation."
— *Henry David Thoreau*

"Be willing to do more than you are paid to do."
— Andrew Carnegie

"Any person who produces less than his very best is cheating. And, as Emerson was fond of pointing out, in the long haul, the only person we really cheat is ourselves."
— Earl Nightingale

"Beware of what you want, for you will surely get it."
— Ralph Waldo Emerson

"The greatest discovery of my generation is that you can change your circumstances by changing your attitudes of mind."
— William James

"I will not accept people saying, 'that's it; that's as good as it gets', and that's the difference. I don't think anything's impossible."
— David Hartman

"Life doesn't have to be the way it always was."
— Jim Rohn

"He who buys what he doesn't need steals from himself."
— Swedish Proverb

"Man is not the creature of circumstances; circumstances are the creatures of man."
— Benjamin Disraelli

"Children begin by loving their parents; as they grow older they judge them; sometimes they forgive them."
— Oscar Wilde

"A wise man makes more opportunities than he finds."
— Francis Bacon

"You are the only one who can use your ability, it is an awesome responsibility."
— Zig Ziglar

"That which holds our attention determines our action."
— *William James*

"Life leaps like a geyser for those who drill through the rock of inertia."
— *Dr. Alexis Carrel*

NOW IS THE TIME

Now is the time.
    Wait not to do the things your heart desires
Until that day when worries are gone and there is time.
    That day is but a fluttering of wings,
Who keeps forever just beyond our reach.
    Now is the time.

Now is the time.
    How often have you missed an opportunity
And did not pause to give it thought or action?
    Let not your golden chances slip by. The door
Once closed, perhaps may open nevermore.
    Now is the time.
— *Karen G. Boswell*

"I've never known a man worth his salt who in the long run, deep down in his heart, didn't appreciate the grind, the discipline."
— *Vince Lombardi*

"I can give you a six-word formula for success: Think things through — then follow through."
— *Edward Vernon Rickenbacker*

"The objective is to win — fairly, squarely, decently, by the rules — but to win."
— *Vince Lombardi*

"My mother drew a distinction between achievement and success. She said that 'achievement is the knowedge that you have studied and worked hard and done the best that is in you. Success is being praised by others and that's nice, too, but not as important or satisfying. Always aim for achievement and forget about success'."
— *Helen Hayes*

A man, who's plane was forced down in the Arctic, had to walk over 800 miles to civilization. While being interviewed, he was asked: "How were you able to walk over 800 miles in the frozen wilderness?" His immediate reply was: "I didn't walk 800 miles. I walked one mile 800 times."
— *Author Unknown*

"None of us know what is ahead...The important thing is to use today wisely and well and face tomorrow eagerly, cheerfully and with the certainty we shall be equal to what it brings."
— *Channing Pollock*

"First say to yourself what you would be; and then do what you have to do."
— *Epictetus*

"Obstacles may not be deterrents. An obstacle can be a sign post indicating the next step toward achievement of your ultimate goal. It is only a stimulus to your ingenuity to devise a way under, around, over or through that obstacle."
— *Author Unknown*

"What people say you cannot do, you try and find out that you can."
— *Henry David Thoreau*

"He who tries something and fails is infinitely greater than he who tries nothing and succeeds."
— *Confucious*

"Four things come not back: The spoken word; The sped arrow; Time past; The neglected opportunity."
— *Omar Ibn*

"Time is the coin of your life. It is the only coin you have and only you can determine how it will be spent. Be careful lest you let other people spend it for you."
— *Carl Sandburg*

"For though we sleep or wake or roam or ride, age fleets the time, it will no man abide."
— *Geoffrey Chaucer*

"Time is nature's way of keeping everything from happening at the same time."
— *Author Unknown*

"Dost thou love life? Then do not squander time, for that is the stuff life is made of."
— *Ben Franklin*

"You can ask me for anything you like except time."
— *Napoleon Bonaparte*

"Remember that man's life lies all within the present, as't were but a hair's breadth of time; as for the rest, the past is gone, the future may never be. Short, therefore, is man's life and narrow is the corner of the earth wherein he dwells."
— *Marcus Aurelius*

"Nothing is impossible; there are ways which lead to everything; and if we had sufficient will we should always have sufficient means."
— *Francois De La Rochefoucauld*

"There is always enough time for the important things. If it's important, I'll make time to do it."
— *Dan Lakein*

"In truth, people can generally make time for what they choose to do; it is not really the time but the will that is lacking."
— *Sir John Lubbock*

"The more we do, the more we can do; the busier we are, the more leisure we have."
— *William Hazlitt*

"Let all things be done decently and in order."
— *Old Testament*

"If you want work well done, select a busy man — the other kind has no time."
— *Elbert Hubbard*

"A place for everything and everything in its place."
— *Samuel Smiles*

"Never spend money before you have it."
— *Thomas Jefferson*

"Resolve not to be poor; whatever you have, spend less."
— *Samuel Johnson*

"Any government, like any family, can, for a year, spend a little more than it earns. But, you and I know, a continuance of that habit means the poorhouse."
— *Franklin D. Roosevelt*

"Every man is the architect of his own fortune."
— *Appius Claudius*

"If your outgo exceeds your income, then your upkeep becomes your downfall."
— *Jim Rohn*

"It's easier to reach the stars when you're not held down by negative attitudes."
— *Author Unknown*

"The biggest mistake you can make is to believe that you are working for someone else."
— *Author Unknown*

"Thrift is care and scruple in the spending of one's means. It is not a virtue and it requires neither skill nor talent."
— *Immanuel Kant*

"He will always be a slave who does not know how to live upon a little."
— *Horace*

"Endure and persist; this pain will turn to your good."
— *Ovid*

"The trick is to make sure you don't die waiting for prosperity to come."
— *Lee Iacocca*

"I believe in the equal opportunity in this country to become as unequal as our capabilities will allow us to become."
— *Don Quess*

"Hit the ball over the fence and you can take your time getting around the bases."
— *John W. Raper*

"The art of getting riches consists very much in thrift. All men are not equally qualified in getting money, but it is the power of everyone alike to practice this virtue."
— *Benjamin Franklin*

"If you keep on doin' what you're doin',
You'll continue gettin' what you're gettin'."
— *Zig Ziglar*

"To be idle and to be poor have always been reproaches and, therefore, every man endeavors with his utmost to hide his poverty from others and his idleness from himself."
— *Samuel Johnson*

"Money is of a prolific, generating nature. Money can beget money and its offspring can beget more."
— *Benjamin Franklin*

"We cannot do everything at once, but we can do something at once."
— *Calvin Coolidge*

"The price of success is much lower than the price of failure."
Zig Ziglar

"The highest reward for a man's toil is not what he gets out of it, but what he becomes by it."
— *John Ruskin*

"Nothing is enough for man to whom enough is too little."
— *Epicurus*

"Duty, then, is the sublimest word in our language. Do your duty in all things. You cannot do more. You should never wish to do less."
— *Robert E. Lee*

"I always remember an epitaph which is in the cemetery at Tombstone, Arizona. It says: 'Here lies Jack Wilson. He done his damnedest.' I think that is the greatest epitaph a man can have — when he gives everything that is in him to do the job he has before him. That is all you can ask of him and that is what I have tried to do."
— *Harry S. Truman*

"Your old men shall dream dreams, your young men shall see visions."
— *Old Testament*

'Success is not so much achievement as achieving. Refuse to join the cautious crowd that plays not to lose; play to win."
— *David J. Mahoney*

"Restlessness is discontent — and discontent is the first necessity of progress. Show me a thoroughly satisfied man and I will show you a failure."
— *Thomas A. Edison*

"Don't be afraid to take a big step when one is indicated. You can't cross a chasm in two small jumps."
— *David Lloyd*

"If we attend continually and promptly to the little that we can do, we shall ere long be surprised to find how little remains that we cannot do."
— *Samuel Butler*

"Laziness travels so slowly that poverty soon overtakes him."
— *Benjamin Franklin*

"Mediocrity is like hitching your life to a cloud instead of a star. Clouds obstruct light and warmth, create worries and doubts, postpone dreams and aspirations. When you are hitched to a cloud, you move with the wind whichever way it blows".
— *Dr. H. Paul Jacobi*

"The world does not pay for what a person knows. But it pays for what a person does with what he knows."
— *Laurence Lee*

"I do not know that knowledge amounts to anything more definite than a novel and grand surprise or a sudden revelation of the inefficiency of all that we have called knowledge before; an indefinite sense of the grandeur and glory of the universe."
— *Henry David Thoreau*

"It is easier to go down a hill than up but the view is from the top."
— *Arnold Bennett*

"All men by nature desire to know."
— *Aristotle*

"You better live your best and act your best and think your best today for today is the sure preparation for tomorrow and all the other tommorrows that follow."
— *Harriet Martineau*

"Man's capacities have never been measured; nor are we to judge of what we can do by any precedents, so little has been tried."
— *Feodor Dostoevski*

"Perhaps the most valuable result of all education is the ability to make yourself do the thing you have to do, when it ought to be done, whether you like it or not; it is the first lesson that ought to be learned; and, however early a man's training begins, it is probably the last lesson that he learns thoroughly."
— *Thomas Henry Huxley*

"What lies behind us and what lies before us are tiny matters compared to what lies within us."
— *Ralph Waldo Emerson*

"I believe in human dignity as the source of national purpose, human liberty as the source of national action, the human heart as the source of national compassion and in the human mind as the source of our inventions and our ideas."
— *John F. Kennedy*

"The absurd man is one who never changes."
— *Auguste Barthelemy*

"You are young, my son, and, as the years go by, time will change and even reverse many of your present opinions. Refrain, therefore, awhile from setting yourself up as a judge of the highest matters."
— *Plato*

"No well-informed person has declared a change of opinion to be inconstancy."
— *James Russell Lowell*

"A teacher affects eternity; he can never tell where his influence stops."
— *Henry Adams*

"Let no youth have any anxiety about the upshot of his education, whatever the line of it may be. If he keeps faithfully busy each hour of the working day, he may safely leave the final result to itself. He can, with perfect certainty, count on waking some fine morning to find himself one of the competent ones of his generation in whatever pursuit he may have singled out."
— *William James*

"The price of greatness is responsibility."
— *Winston Churchill*

"Take time to deliberate but, when the time for action has arrived, stop thinking and go in."
— *Napoleon Bonaparte*

"The relation between superiors and inferiors is like that between the wind and the grass. The grass must bend when the wind blows over it."
— *Confucious*

"Let every man be swift to hear, slow to speak."
— *New Testament*

"It is the province of knowledge to speak and it is the privilege of wisdom to listen."
— *Oliver Wendell Holmes*

You've got to have the goods, my boy,
    If you would finish strong;
A bluff may work a little while,
    But not for very long;
A line of talk all by itself
    Will seldom see you through;
You've got to have the goods, my boy,
    And nothing else will do.

The fight is pretty stiff, my boy,
    I'd call it rather tough,
And all along the route are wrecks
    Of those who tried to bluff —
They could not back their lines of talk,
    To meet the final test,
You've got to have the goods, my boy,
    And that's no idle jest.
        — *Author Unknown*

"Others judge us by what we have done. We judge ourselves by what we are capable of doing."
        — *Longfellow*

"If you can do it, that ain't braggin'."
        — *Dizzy Dean*

"Men give me some credit for genius. All the genius I have lies in this: When I have a subject in hand, I study it profoundly. Day and night it is before me. I explore it in all its bearings. My mind becomes pervaded with it. Then the effort which I made the people are pleased to call the 'fruit of genius'. It is the fruit of labor and thought."
        — *Alexander Hamilton*

"A man must consider what a realm he abdicates when he becomes a conformist."
        — *Ralph Waldo Emerson*

"A tough lesson in life that one has to learn is that not everybody wishes you well."
        — *Dan Rather*

"The great thing in this world is not so much where we are but in what direction we are moving."
        — *Oliver Wendell Holmes*

"Make it a point to do something every day that you don't want to do. This is the golden rule for acquiring the habit of doing your duty without pain."
— *Mark Twain*

Andrew Carnegie was once asked what he considered most important in industry: labor, capital or brains. With a laugh, Carnegie replied: "Which is the most important leg of a three-legged stool?"

"There are no limitations to the mind except those we acknowledge."
— *Napoleon Hill*

"The roots of education are bitter but the fruit is sweet."
— *Aristotle*

A woman rushed up to famed violinist Fritz Kreisler, after a concert, and cried: "I'd give my life to play as beautifully as you do." Kreisler replied, "I did."

"Get happiness out of your work or you may never know what happiness is."
— *Elbert Hubbard*

"A profession is a personal thing that man acquires. It cannot be inherited. It cannot be bequeathed. Only he who, having made the decision, puts to use that knowledge and skill, with all his ability and complete dedication of purpose, can be truly called a professional."
— *R. E. Onstad*

"If you have built castles in the air, your work need not be lost; that is where they shold be. Now put the foundations under them."
— *Henry David Thoreau*

"The opportunity isn't as rare as the ability to recognize it."
— *Jack Howell, Jr.*

"You gain strength, courage and confidence by every experience in which you really stop to look fear in the face. You are able to say to yourself, 'I have lived through this horror. I can take the next thing that comes along'. You must do the thing you think you cannot do."
— *Eleanor Roosevelt*

"My life seems like one long obstacle course, with me as the chief obstacle."
— *Jack Paar*

"The man who starts out with the idea of getting rich won't succeed: you must have a larger ambition. There is no mystery in business success. If you do each day's task successfully, stay faithful within the natural operations of commercial law and keep your head clear, you will come out all right."
— *John D. Rockefeller*

"The higher men climb, the longer their working day. And any young man with a streak of idleness in him may better make up his mind at the beginning that mediocrity will be his lot. Without immense, sustained effort, he will not climb high. And even though fortune or chance were to leave him high, he would not stay there. For to stay at the top is almost harder than to get there. There are not office hours for leaders."
— *Cardinal Gibbons*

"He who would leap high must take a long run."
— *Danish Proverb*

"In effect, the quality of a man's life is in direct proportion to his commitment to excellence regardless of his field of endeavor."
— *Vince Lombardi*

"I believe most people don't know what they can do. Look, what's the difference between Vince Lombardi and a high school football coach? It's a question of getting a little more precision."
— *Henry Kissinger*

"The secret of greatness is simple: Do better work than any other man in your field — and keep on doing it."
— *Wilfred A. Peterson*

"Aim at perfection in everything though, in most things, it is unattainable; however, they who aim at it, and persevere, will come much nearer to it than those whose laziness and despondency make them give it up as unattainable."
— Lord Chesterfield

"Perfect freedom is reserved for the man who lives by his own work and in that work does what he wants to do."
— Robin George Collingwood

"A man who qualifies himself well for his calling, never fails of employment."
— Thomas Jefferson

"Enjoy when you can and endure when you must."
— Goethe

"Success is...trendy word. Don't aim for success if you want it; just do what you love and it will come naturally."
— David Frost

"I believe the true road to preeminent success in any line is to make yourself master of that line."
— Andrew Carnegie

"It's a shame that more often non-achievers harbor jealousies and anger toward achievers than to give praise and thanks. For, without the achievers, the non-achievers would have no free lunch."
— Dawn R. Bence

"Be not afraid of greatness. Some are born great, some achieve greatness and some have greatness thrust upon them."
— Shakespeare

"Equality, uniformity, mediocrity — that is the philosophy of failure."
— Dr. H. Paul Jacobi

"When your work speaks for itself, don't interrupt."
— Henry J. Kaiser

"Try not to become a man of success but rather to become a man of value."

— *Albert Einstein*

"It's a good idea to step out of the line every once in a while and look up ahead to see if the line is going where we want it to go."

— *Author Unknown*

"Keep changing. When you're through changing, you're through."

— *Bruce Barton*

"Some people get to the mountain top and think how pretty it is, but the real achievers get to the mountain top and immediately start looking around for another mountain to climb."

— *Fran Tarkinton*

"Don't try to master too many things."

— *William McKinley*

"If I were to try and read, much less answer, all the attacks made on me, this shop might as well be closed for any other business. I do the very best I know how — the very best I can, and I mean to keep doing so until the end. If the end brings me out all right, what is said against me won't amount to anything. If the end brings me out wrong, then ten angels swearing I was right would make no difference."

— *Abraham Lincoln*

"Don't just learn how to earn. Learn how to live. Learn how to enjoy what you have while getting what you want."

— *Jim Rohn*

"The best of a book is not in the thought that it contains but in the thought that it suggests. Just as the charm of music dwells not in the tones but in the echoes of our hearts."

— *Oliver Wendell Holmes*

LIFE CHOICES is Published by:
EMPIRE COMMUNICATIONS
5818 N. 7th Street, Suite #103,
Phoenix, Arizona 85014
DAN S. KENNEDY, *Publisher and Editor-In-Chief*

EMPIRE COMMUNICATIONS CORPORATION publishes a varied selection of books, manuals, audio-cassettes, home study courses and newsletters on self-imorovement, business and financial topics.
A Catalog of Empire Publications is available free, on request, by writing to the address listed above or by calling, toll-free, 1-800-223-7180.